Am I Ever Going to Get Out of Here?

Ben Mathes

Parson's Porch & Company

Am I Ever Going to Get Out of Here?

Parson's Porch Books

Am I Ever Going to Get Out of Here?

ISBN: Softcover 978-1-951472-35-1

Copyright © 2015 by Ben Mathes

All rights reserved. No part of this book may be reproduced or transmitted in any form or by any means, electronic or mechanical, including photocopying, recording, or by any information storage and retrieval system, without permission in writing from the publisher.

To order additional copies of this book, contact:

Parson's Porch Books

1-423-475-7308

www.parsonsporch.com

Parson's Porch Books is an imprint of Parson's Porch & Company (PP&C) in Cleveland, Tennessee. PP&C is an innovative organization which raises money by publishing books of noted authors, representing all genres. All donations from contributors and profits from publishing are shared with the poor.

Table of Contents

Foreword	7
Preface	9
Am I Ever Going to Get Out of Here?	11
From Tongi to Karomtola	36
How Then Shall We Live?	48
How to Survive in this World	63
I Hope I Don't Forget This	76
I've Had Enough	88
Not Just Yet	99
One Day Closer	108
Prepared to Praise	122
Rejoice and Be Glad	132
The Requirements of Love	145
The Cart before the Horse	156
The First Thing I Forget	166
The Formula for Life	175
The Joyful Accomplishment of Faith	187
The Unknown God	197
Three Words	207
Remember Who You Are!	223

Foreword

Rev. Dr. Ben Mathes is one of the most engaging, thrilling, and articulate storytellers around today. His words bring you into the story, and the story and its characters come off the page and into your livingroom as you read.

For over 35 years, Ben has travelled the world loving people in the name of Jesus. For the past 20 years that has been through Rivers of the World (ROW) www.row.org, the organization he founded. To read the pages of this book is to walk alongside Ben in the jungles of places like Venezuela, Peru, and the Congo. You'll ride with him in the boat as he travels the Amazon River, the Mamano, the Oroso, and many others. His stories will take you to places you will likely never have the opportunity to visit (and to some places you'd never want to visit either) as he has reached out to provide loving care for God's people for 4 decades.

To know Ben is to love him. For 18 years, I've had the privilege of calling Ben my friend. We've walked together through war, disease, and famine that you will likely never experience beyond the pages of this book. We've experienced great joy as lives have been transformed and hope has been restored where it had been lost for centuries. We've laughed, cried, and prayed together, and God has used Ben Mathes to literally change the world.

Reading this book will be like sitting in a pew while Ben shares stories of his life in a sermon, or at a table with him over tea as he captivates you with the unfolding of his life's experiences. By the end of the journey you'll be different, and you'll likely want to make a greater difference as well.

ENJOY!

Mike Reinsel, Executive Director, ROW

Preface

Thanks for reading this little book of sermons. It was written a lot like I talk—so I hope it made sense, did not repeat too often, and has reminded you of the fun we've had over the years!

Even though I am Presbyterian, I was educated in part by a Baptist minister, who always told me, "Whatever else you say, leave people with one thing; HOPE in Christ!" That's always made sense to me, and I pray always guided me.

In 35 years of travelling God's world and His church, I usually only saw you once a year. During our visits, I would share what was new from the mission fields we served, and then preach about it.

As an audience, you were always kind and complimentary—thank you—It kept me going through good and not-so-good times in life! My family grew up in your churches. You prayed for us as we served, whether that was on a river in the Congo, or the Euphrates in Iraq. Your church suppers fed us physically, your prayers sustained us spiritually, and the Mathes' are forever thankful for you!

My hope in Christ is that you will know what I tried to share—that God loves you so much that He sent His Son to die for you—that you can be strong, you can be brave, you can grow past any failure, and that God has a purpose for your life, so rejoice and have fun as you live it!!

God bless you. You stay strong, and God bless America.

Ben

The Old Man of ROW

Am I Ever Going to Get Out of Here?

"Only let your manner of life be worthy of the gospel of Christ, so that whether I come and see you or am absent, I may hear of you that you standing firm in one spirit, with one mind striving side by side for the faith of the gospel, and not frightened in anything by your opponents."
Philippians 1:27-28a

Chad was one of those special people who showed up in Zaire just to help us. A college age student from South Carolina, he was blessed with strength, intelligence, and the ability to fix absolutely anything! Chad had given two years of his life serving the Lord in Zaire.

We became fast friends on one of my trips to that country and had an adventure that began in Bulape. While visiting Dr. Ken and Nancy McGill of the Bulape Hospital, a runner arrived from the village of Lodi, located approximately 75 kilometers through the bush. He had come to deliver an important message. It seemed that three months earlier, a truck belonging to the Presbyterian Church of Zaire had fallen from a ferryboat crossing the Sankuru River. The ferryboat operator had been drunk, and he ran his boat onto a sand bar, and it capsized. Several people drowned, and the truck was presumed lost.

The truck was pulled from the river, and now it was sitting on the bank. In order to save this large and valuable vehicle, it would have to be attended to immediately. Chad was just the man. With his knowledge of vehicles, he was chosen to head the "expeditionary task to Lodi!" The task force included Chad and me.

We loaded tools, diesel fuel, oil, and a spare battery into the Land Cruiser. We left Bulape with scant directions, and the best prayers of the McGill's. Our goal was to travel 75 kilometers through the forest to the village of Lodi. At that point, we hoped to dismantle the truck, clean its parts, put it back together, and pray the engine would start. With that bold assignment, we began our journey. It took us three hours to reach the major metropolitan area of Mushenge. From there we continued down to the river and to the village of Lodi.

In Lodi, we were royally greeted by Chief Bokongo, and he took us directly to the truck. We were overwhelmed when we saw the remains of the massive truck which was a World War II German troop transport truck. The truck appeared to be in pretty good condition.

Undaunted, Chad went right to work. He began emptying the fuel tank, the transmission, transfer cases, and the engine. River water freely flowed beneath the truck! I had no idea that an engine block could hold so much water. We took as much of the engine apart as possible, cleaned the various points and parts, and put it back together. Eventually, we refilled every space that had previously been occupied by river water—oil went into the proper places, grease filled the transmission, and diesel filled the fuel tank.

Chad spent the next hour or so fine-tuning the engine, replacing the battery, and making the necessary connections. When he finished, he climbed into the driver's seat. "Oh, no!" he proclaimed, "Ben, all of the instruments are in German! I cannot read German! What in the world are we going to do?!" Thank goodness, one of the languages I studied in college was German. I climbed into the truck with the best hopes of being able to save the day.

Unfortunately, the instructions were written in German script. This is difficult to read at best, and for me, almost impossible to understand. I looked at the mass of confusing words before me, and prayed that the Lord would simply show me the word "on." I looked around, picked the appropriate word, flipped the switch, and casually said, "Okay, Chad, try it now." I was not about to let my new friend know that I was absolutely lost!

Chad returned to the truck, pushed a few buttons, turned the key, and rejoiced with me as the truck started. It seemed the entire village was clapping and cheering with us. Chad moved the vehicle forward a few feet, and allowed the engine to idle for a while. We had been successful! Chad would now return to Bulape, and I followed in the Land Cruiser.

Through the helpful interpretation of a local merchant, I learned of the village of Bolombo, which was located several kilometers up the river. Across the river was the home of Chief Ekongusamu and part of the Dekesee Tribe. From all indications, this village had not been visited by a missionary in many years. I was curious.

I found two little boys with a dugout canoe who were willing to escort me to the village of Bolombo. Chad agreed to return to Bulape on his own, and I promised that I would arrive the next day or so. Both of us were rather concerned that I was heading off on this adventure.

The people of Lodi speak Lingala. At the time, I spoke very little Tshiluba, and absolutely nothing more than a greeting in Lingala. Nevertheless, this seemed like a wonderful opportunity for an adventure, so off I went!

A dugout canoe in Zaire is less than three feet wide. I stand six feet tall, and weigh close to 200 pounds. My guides were two little boys about 10 years old. (Try to imagine the sight of a large American squatting in a dugout canoe, while two little boys did their best to paddle their oversized load upstream!) We traveled for several kilometers, and laughed at each other on the way. The little boys and I could communicate only with sign language, smiles, and the anticipation of a great adventure. They knew they were taking me to Bolombo. I knew they were taking me somewhere!

We ultimately parked on the far side of the river. The little boys pulled the canoe onto the shore and rapidly produced small fishhooks and a line. I watched them deftly toss the fishhooks and lines into the river. In a matter of minutes, they had five or six small fish that looked like our American bream.

Am I Ever Going to Get Out of Here?

We built a fire and the little boys threw the fish into the fire. I noticed they had not cleaned the fish. They simply allowed their catch to be burned charcoal black on both sides. Once the fire had died, they removed the remains of the fish from the ashes. They handed me two fish, and I watched as they slid their portion of our meal into their pockets. Not wanting to look out of place I casually did the same thing.

With much laughing and pointing, we headed off through the bush and toward the forest. Along the way, we passed through a large sandy area. I surmised that this must be the overflow area for the river during the rainy season. We spotted several large birds that looked like flamingos. The little boys produced slingshots from their back pockets and began their stalk. I adjusted my camera and fell in behind the hunters.

As we approached the birds, it became obvious that the birds could run faster than we could. With shouting and hollering, we chased our targets, and the little boys launched their rocks from their slingshots. Unscathed, the birds flew into the forest and out of our way.

On the far side of the sandy area was a black water swamp. I had just watched a movie called *Star Wars*. In that movie, one of the characters is sucked under by a large monster in a garbage dump. As we waded in black water over our knees, I could not help but expect to be sucked under by some unknown creature. We were all barefooted and wearing shorts. I had on a polo shirt and a safari vest. We were adequately dressed for the occasion of swamp crossing.

Having arrived safely on the other side of the swamp, I breathed a sigh of relief.

The temperature dropped noticeably under the canopy of the rain forest. Though the sun was shining, I was amazed at how dark it was in the forest. Everything was covered with dew. With each step we took, an animal screamed and ran off under the bushes. It was both frightening and thrilling at the same time.

Over the years, I have been in several tense situations. I have faced my fears by reciting the 23rd Psalm or by singing hymns like, *A Mighty Fortress Is Our God*. And to be honest, I have even found courage by singing the southern hymn called *Dixie!*

It is hard to imagine what we must have looked like that day in the rain forest. With one little boy in front of me, and the other one in the back of me, I sang at the top of my lungs, "Well, I wish I was in the land of cotton...!"

After several choruses of my favorite song, I attempted to whistle to relieve the tension. I whistled a sound and the boys would whistle back to me. We tried our best to hide our fear.

The boy leading the way let out the loudest scream I have ever heard! As any adult would do, I immediately reached down and snatched the boy back into my arms. His friend had grabbed the back of my leg and was peering around my side. I looked up in time to greet a stranger on our path.

We froze. The stranger in our midst had a bow and arrow in his hands. He had drawn his bow and was pointing directly at me with a long and sharp arrow. My mind was racing. I was not sure how I should respond to this threat. I slowly moved the boy in front of me to the back. I was not going to let him hurt either of them if I could help it.

We stood staring at each other for what seemed like an eternity. I finally remembered that I was armed. Very slowly, and yet with all the confidence I could muster, I pointed my camera, with its long telephoto lens at the stranger, and said in English, "Do not move!" I can remember thinking to myself, "This is great. This fellow is going to kill me, but at least I will get his picture!"

Another eternity slowly passed. He was not going to move, and neither was I. I was frozen to the ground! My mind continued to race, and it finally dawned on me that perhaps this man understood French. The traders who worked the river spoke French. In my best French, I asked him if he would like a photograph. A smile came across his face. He turned to one side, raised his bow and arrow, drew the arrow back, turned his head toward me, and gave me a large smile. I took his picture and breathed a huge sigh of relief.

Please do not misunderstand. This man was simply a hunter from the village. He came upon us in the forest, and he was as surprised by our presence as we were by his presence. Having had his photograph taken, he joyfully went on his way.

We continued on to the village, and were surprised to learn that our friend had obviously informed the citizens of Bolombo that a white man was coming. We literally came around a curve in the path and found the entire village lining the way to greet us.

The only word I knew in Lingala was, "Mbote." That is a general greeting. The villagers obviously knew that word and responded in kind. In addition, they seemed to have an unusual way of letting you know that you are welcome; they laugh at you.

It is an awkward feeling when your friends laugh at you. It is extremely awkward when an entire village of strangers laugh at you. You feel as if you are either over or under dressed for the occasion, or you are simply in the wrong place at the wrong time. Nevertheless, I entered the village. I spoke to myself out loud in English. I remember saying to myself, "Boy, isn't it great to be here?! Yes, it is so much fun to be here. Uh huh—it is so good to see everyone. Boy I wish my friends could see me now. I cannot believe I am here. This is so much fun!"

I entered the village common area and was immediately approached by several elderly women. Not quite five feet tall, they approached me as slowly and properly as they could. I smiled and stood very still. The oldest one approached me first. She slowly raised her right hand with her index finger extended. She rubbed her finger across my cheek, attempting to rub the white from my skin. She removed it very slowly, walked back her friends, and showed her finger to her companions. They all giggled.

Once again, fear came creeping up my spine. I froze. I could feel the presence of someone at my back. You cannot help but be afraid in times like this. I honestly did not know if I should run, if I should turn around quickly, or what! Thank goodness, my feet were frozen in their tracks, and I had no choice in the matter.

I felt the warmth of a human hand reaching to my neck. I remained unable to move. I felt three or four fingers touch the hair at the base of my head. Very slowly, the little fingers began to play with my hair. I turned my head to the right, and looked into the eyes of the very elderly woman who was exploring the back of my head. With my best Humphrey Bogart imitation, I simply said, "Hello sweetheart." The lady screamed and ran to join her laughing companions.

My tour guides appeared and ushered me into the presence of Chief Ekongusamu. An elderly man sitting on the ground with a large walking stick, he barely looked up when I was introduced. He was not impressed. He did, however, motion for me to have a seat. I sat on the ground beside him and began attempting to explain who I was and why I was in his village.

He basically dismissed my attempt at conversation as a woman arrived in our midst carrying a small porcelain bowl. With expected propriety, she lowered the bowl first to the Chief. He took a handful of the contents and placed it in his mouth. It became obvious to me that we were going to share a meal. I refused to look into the bowl. I simply recalled the words I had heard before, "Where you lead I will follow, what you feed I will swallow."

I took a handful of the food and began to pitch it into my mouth. Unfortunately, I looked down right before I ate. In my hand were half a dozen smoked caterpillars—complete with legs! I threw them into my mouth as if they were potato chips, and I ate this way every day! They tasted something like leather shoelaces. They had been smoked over an open fire and were as tough as they could be. The good news is that if you chew anything long enough, it will eventually go away. I chewed and chewed and attempted to regain my composure.

The woman who had served us the caterpillars returned with a large wicker basket. Again, she politely lowered the basket to the Chief. This time, I decided to watch more closely. The Chief put his hand in the basket and waved it back and forth. I decided that the basket must contain hot meat of some kind. He took something in hand and pitched it into his mouth. I was not afraid. The woman lowered the basket to me, and I became afraid! The large basket was almost completely filled with live African termites.

Termites in Zaire have two things over American termites—size and pincers. They are over an inch long and have pincers that can inflict a great deal of pain on unsuspecting eaters. However, I noticed that the Chief had fanned his hand over the crowd of termites. Apparently, he was trying to get the advantage on one. He then very swiftly threw the bug into his mouth and ended its misery. I decided that as fast as I can talk, I would undoubtedly be able to bite a termite. I batted them around with my hand, grabbed one by the end and threw it into my mouth. So far, so good.

Unfortunately, things went downhill rapidly from that point. The bug landed on my cheek and bit me!

I could not believe the pain! I continued to bite at the biting bug and roll on the ground using what I call "South Georgia" language. The Chief was amused by my antics. He actually smiled and then started laughing. Tragically, the woman who served me grew concerned. She pulled another termite out of the basket, smashed it in the palm of her hand with her finger, and wiped its remains into the palm of my hand.

Not wanting to seem impolite, I then scraped the remains from my palm into my mouth with my teeth. I chewed as politely as possible, hoping that I would not get ill in front of my host. I made a great mistake at this point; I looked the woman in the eye and said, "Bimpe." To the best of my knowledge that is a Tshiluba word which means "good." I am afraid the woman understood me. She began an assembly line—pluck, smush, wipe, scrape. I ate enough termites on that day to feed half of the Dekesee Tribe!

Thinking that our meal was done, my stomach and I began to relax. Unfortunately, the meal was not complete until the meat had been served.

My hunter friend had managed to successfully shoot a large black monkey. It was not a chimpanzee, but a monkey that I had not previously seen.

There is an old belief that still remains among remote tribes in Zaire. When a hunter kills an animal, his skin must first be scorched off so that his spirit will not tell the other animals what happened to him. Keeping with tradition, the villagers took the monkey and threw it in the fire. It burned something like the fish that were still in my pocket. Once the monkey was adequately burned, it was pulled from the fire with a large stick.

Being the guest of honor has certain advantages. However, those advantages are determined by your location and the culture of the tribe. That did not hold true in this part of Zaire. Being the guest of honor apparently meant that I got the best piece of monkey. The Chief had the hands of the monkey removed and handed them to me on a small metal plate. I was overjoyed to say the least! I removed the ever-present Swiss army knife from my pocket and did my best to cut up the hands and act as if I were eating a little monkey meat. It was by no means the best meal I have ever had.

After our luncheon, the Chief gave me a tour of the village. It was obvious that at some point in time, Roman Catholic missionaries had constructed a clinic in this part of the forest. I made a note of that, took a picture of the clinic, and ultimately began my return journey to Lodi.

While in route to the river, the boys became hungry. At this point, our blackened fish were produced. We sat on a tree stump by the side of the river. I learned to take the fish, turn it upside down, and crack it open with my fingers. After removing as many of the unpleasant insides as possible, we scraped the remaining meat from the fish with our fingernails. Believe it or not, it was not altogether unpleasant. In fact, cooked fish was somewhat more acceptable to my stomach than monkey, termites and caterpillars.

We loaded into the dugout canoe, returned to the village of Lodi, and I rejoined my friends at the Bulape Hospital. However, that was not the end of my adventure?

No, not hardly! This is actually where the adventure begins. Approximately two days later, I became desperately ill. I had a classic case of amoebic dysentery. It began as expected. Cramps and diarrhea was the norm. I spent more time running to the outhouse, than running away from it! In tropical countries, dysentery often flushes the antimalarial prophylactic out of your system. My body's Chloroquine supply was rapidly depleting and a raging fever set in.

It appeared that I contracted malaria on top of my dysentery. Our medical missionaries became concerned.

I recall getting sick in the middle of the night. The volume of fluid I was passing from my body was much greater than the volume going in. I was very weak, and my urine had turned almost black.

As I came out of the bathroom one night, I was greeted by Dr. Walt Hull, the OB/GYN physician of the Good Shepherd Hospital in Kananga, Zaire. He was not very encouraging. "Ben, it sounds like you have cholera," Walt said too seriously. "Great, Walt, you have made my night," I tried to respond. I returned to my bed, and another fitful night passed.

As quickly as possible, I was loaded into a truck and sent to the Good Shepherd Hospital. This was home base. I stayed in my room at the guesthouse for four or five days. I was unable to eat anything except a mango and banana. I kept thinking that I would feel better. I had taken what Dr. McGill called "Chloroquine cure." Massive doses of the antimalarial medicine were fed to me in pill form. That must be one of the greatest miracles of modern medicine. Within 20 minutes after taking the medications, the fever lifted and never returned. I am so very grateful for those pills!

My last night at the Good Shepherd Hospital was rather difficult. Dr. Hull appeared at my bedside, and in his best physician manner said, "Look Mathes, you can die anywhere you want to. However, you are not going to die on us, it would look bad. Get out of Africa!"

With that kind of wonderful support, I tried to pass the night as peacefully as possible. I was ultimately shipped out of Zaire and sent to Brussels to live or die. I later learned that I had gotten ill not because of the bugs or the monkey—I became ill because of the hands that fed me. One must be very careful when one is visiting other countries and other cultures.

Let me go back and talk in greater detail about my last night in Zaire. So many questions were going through my mind. Was I going to survive? Would I ever see my family again? Am I ever going to get out of here?! The fear of being desperately ill in a faraway country is very real. While our medical missionaries do an outstanding job, they simply do not have the resources available to them that can be found in the United States.

Once I finished worrying about myself, I began to think of our missionaries. While my sickness was something new to me, it was an everyday occurrence to those who live in other countries. Faced not only with sickness, but also with the differences of race, culture, distance, and lifestyles, I felt great empathy for those called by God to serve in distant lands.

I could not help but wonder what goes through the mind of a missionary when they face trial and turmoil. Do they wonder about those of us serving Christ in America? Do they wonder if we ever think about them, or actually place ourselves in their shoes? I know that is a difficult task, and I also know that I am thankful that a Bible was placed next to my bed in Zaire.

I began flipping through familiar pages and passages looking for words of comfort. It often happens as we search the Word of God, we find something that speaks not only to our own hearts, but also speaks to others as well. The verse I found which best summarizes my feelings were from Paul's Epistle to the church at Philippi.

Written while Paul was in a Roman prison, some believe it to be his last communication. He suffered martyrdom soon after writing the Epistle of Joy, as the letter to the Philippians is known.

In spite of being concerned with looking his own death in the eye, Paul was able to write the passage found in Philippians 1:27-28(a) (ESV),

> *"Only let your manner of life be worthy of the gospel of Christ, so that whether I come and see you or am absent, I may hear of you that you are standing firm in one spirit, with one mind, striving side by side for the faith of the gospel, and not frightened in anything by your opponents."*

What encouraging and powerful words! As I meditated upon them, it became apparent to me that Paul was not only giving words of strength and power to his friends in the Church, but was also describing for us the traits necessary for Christians who want to change the world. Let us examine what Paul has to say.

As I travel the world, I always have in my possession two important pieces of identification. One is my United States passport. This identifies me as a citizen of the United States, who is protected by our laws, and guaranteed all the right and privileges of American citizenship. The other is my Bible. This identifies me as a citizen of the Kingdom of God and describes for me all the rights and privileges of citizenship in His Kingdom. As Paul discusses, living our lives in a manner worthy of the gospel of Christ, he is more accurately describing our citizenship in the Kingdom of God. What does this mean?

Again, as I travel from country to country, I notice very often that people of my race all look alike. At first glance, it is very difficult to tell any of us apart. I could be identified as someone who is British, French, or basically European. It would be hard to distinguish me from anyone else. However, in times of necessity, I am able to proclaim myself as being a citizen of the United States of America.

In the same way, Christians and non-Christians look alike. In our everyday world, it is difficult to tell one from the other. It is not until a time of crisis that our citizenship is declared.

Consider it for a moment. As life ambles on, the majority of us include our relationship with Jesus Christ in our lives in only a perfunctory manner. It is not until a death in the family, or some similar family crisis, that our "god" becomes apparent.

What do you do during life's most difficult moments? Do you get in your car and drive as fast as possible? Do you head for the local mall and spend money on yourself? Do you eat? In times of trouble do you turn to alcohol or drugs? When things get their most difficult, do you react by running away from the problems, looking after only yourself? In times of trouble, do you get on your knees and seek God's peace and direction?

In order to ascertain the basic belief system of an individual, watch them during the most difficult times of their life. If they can continue on with their heads held high in spite of a crumbling world, you can rest assured that their hope is built on nothing less than Jesus Christ.

To live as a citizen of the Kingdom of God is to also claim these other words written by Paul,

> "No, in all these things we are more than conquerors through Him who loved us. For I am sure that neither death nor life, nor angels nor rulers, nor things present nor things to come, nor powers, nor height nor depth, nor anything else in all creation, will be able to separate us from the love of God and Christ Jesus our Lord."
> (Romans 8:37-39, ESV)

When Paul says that he is sure of these things, he is actually speaking of the bold confidence that comes from knowing that we are, in fact, members of the very Kingdom of God, and nothing can remove from us that citizenship.

Such citizenship carries us through the days of joy and normalcy in life. Such citizenship grants each of us courage to endure our own personal suffering. Such citizenship enables us to look at the world with creative visions and to conquer the impossible. How many times have I heard it said, "That simply cannot be done? These people are too poor, too corrupt, or too ignorant. That is only a dream." How silly!

If that were true, then there would be no electricity at the Good Shepherd Hospital in Zaire. Going against the lack of vision by many, more than 100 men worked for over five years to complete one of the largest privately funded hydroelectric plants in Africa. In order to complete the task, high power lines and water pipe had to be placed in a ditch four feet deep. The ditch was dug by hand. The ditch was two and one half miles long! As citizens of the Kingdom of God, we are called to live our lives in a manner, which proclaims to one and all, "I can do all things through Christ who strengthens me." (Philippians 4:13, NKJV)

John Jackson is a Hunger Action Enabler in the Presbytery of Central Florida. He wrote a beautifully moving poem called, "The Face of God."[1]

> *The line was long, but moving briskly.*
> *And in that line, at the very end,*
> *stood a young girl about twelve years of age.*
> *She waited patiently as those at the front of that long line received a little rice, some canned goods or a little fruit.*
> *Slowly but surely she was getting closer to the front of that line, closer to the food.*
> *From time to time she would glance across the street.*
> *She did not notice the growing concern on the faces of those distributing the food.*
> *The food was running out.*
> *Their anxiety began to show, but she did not notice.*
> *Her attention seemed always to focus on three figures under the trees across the street.*
> *At long last she stepped forward to get her food. But the only thing left was a lonely banana.*

---

[1] NOTE: according to one source on the Internet, this poem is attributed as such: by John Jackson, *Indianapolis Star*; a newspaper photographer was sent to Ecuador in 1987 to cover the earthquake that devastated much of the country. In the midst of such catastrophic suffering, he witnessed a simple scene of compassion.

> *The workers were almost ashamed to tell her that was all that was left.*
> *She did not seem to mind getting that solitary banana.*
> *Quietly she took the precious fruit and ran across the street where three small children waited—perhaps*
> *her sisters and a brother.*
> *Very deliberately she peeled the banana and very carefully divided the banana into three equal parts.*
> *Placing the precious food in the eager hands of those three younger ones—one for you, one for you, one for you—*
> *she then sat down and licked the inside of that banana peel.*
> *In that moment I swear I saw the face of God.*

John is describing the words of Paul when he exhorted the Philippian Church to,

> *"Stand firm in one spirit, with one mind, striving side by side for the faith of the Gospel."*
> (Philippians 1:27b)

Paul is talking about the unity of the Church and our commitment to stand beside each other in times of trial, joy, hunger, famine, war, and peace. If we are to change the world for Jesus Christ, we must join arms as believers around the earth and combine our forces in an all-out effort to conquer sin and evil, wherever it may be found. By ourselves, we can only do a few things.

Imagine the power and the possibilities if all of the Christians in the United States decided they had had enough of the suffering in this world! Imagine the possibilities that could come from a concerted multi-denominational effort to finally eradicate polio, dirty water, malnutrition, witchcraft, and voodoo from the face of the earth! As the innocent child in John Jackson's poem demonstrates, unity and commitment require sacrifice. The oldest child could have kept the entire banana for herself, but out of her commitment to those around her, she was able to eat only that which was left from feeding the younger ones.

If you were that hungry, what would you have done? Would you have kept that banana for yourself? Would you have claimed that it was yours, and yours alone?

No, that little girl demonstrated not only her citizenship in the Kingdom of God, not only her sense of commitment and unity to those she loved, but a delightful sense of courage as well. As we continue to discuss the possibility of changing the world for Christ, I can think of no better words than Paul's, when he said, "Not frightened in anything by your opponents." (Philippians 1:28a)

When I first read those words to my seven-year-old son, Adam, he asked me if that meant he should not be afraid of the haunted house in a local amusement park! We laughed, and I assured him that I too was scared by that haunted house. Paul is talking about a different kind of fear—fear brought to Christians by those who oppose Jesus Christ and His Lordship in this world.

There is a very real distinction to be made at this point. Things that go bump in the night can frighten any of us. However, it is the unnecessary fear brought to us by those who wish to challenge our beliefs and our ways of life that is really unnecessary fear. We are to remind ourselves constantly that, as believers in Jesus Christ, He is on our side, and therefore, no one can be against us.

The first Presbyterian missionaries to the Belgium Congo were William Sheppard, a black man, and Samuel Lapsley, a white man. They traveled to the Congo in 1890. When they arrived at the port of Matadi, they were greeted with an awesome sight. In the words of William Sheppard, let me describe the cemetery for missionaries who had died in service in that frightening part of the world.

> *"In Great Britain, Sweden, and America, they were told that the climate was deadly; that they would be pelted by the rains, scorched by the sun, and murdered by the natives. Yet, in the full knowledge of these conditions, and with hearts imbued with a spirit of God, they went forth on their mission of love. A kiss upon the cheek, a mingling of tears, a wave of the handkerchief, and they were off on their errand for their King. Emaciated by deadly fevers, pelted by tropical storms, stung by the tsetse flies fresh from the lazaretto of misery, fatigued and footsore from many a trap, they have laid themselves down in this pleasant dale 'til He comes."*

Imagine the courage it took to head off to darkest Africa. This was a land of which so little was known. Of the first 150 missionaries to travel to the Congo, over one-third of them perished in their efforts, and yet they continued on. They continued to come from Christian nations around the world to carry the gospel of Jesus Christ into the very depths of Hell. Because of their efforts, the Church was established, souls were saved, and lives were made whole through their unselfish courageous efforts. I suppose William Sheppard summarizes his feelings best in a poem he wrote called, "The Cross."

> *God laid upon my back a grievous load,*
> *A heavy cross to bear along the road;*
> *I staggered on, till lo! One weary day,*
> *An angry lion leaped across my way.*
> *I prayed to God, and swift at His command*
> *The cross became a weapon in my hand;*
> *It slew my raging enemy, and then*
> *It leaped upon my back a cross again!*
> *I faltered many a league, until at length,*
> *Groaning, I fell and found no further strength.*
> *I cried, "O God! I am so weak and lame,"*
> *And swift the cross a winged staff became.*
> *It swept me on until I retrieved my loss,*
> *Then leaped upon my back again a cross.*
> *I reached a desert; on its burning track*
> *I still perceived the cross upon my back.*
> *No shade was there, and in the burning sun*
> *I sank me down and thought my day was done;*
> *But God's grace works many a sweet surprise.*
> *The cross became a tree before mine eyes.*
> *I slept, awoke, and had the strength of ten,*
> *Then felt the cross upon my back again.*
> *And thus through all my days, from that to this,*
> *The cross, my burden, has become my bliss;*

> *Nor shall I ever lay my burden down,*
> *For God shall one day make my cross a crown.*

A legend comes to us from the war torn France of 50 years ago. While charging into battle, a veteran soldier comes upon a much younger member of the Army. The young man is scared. He was curled up into a ball and was shaking with fear. With the wisdom of many trials, the older soldier looks to the younger man and says, "Come, my son, let us do a fine thing for France." Together, they charged into battle and to their destiny.

In a very real sense, Christians are called to fill their hearts and souls with the courage that comes from a personal relationship with Jesus Christ. We are called to stop in the battlefield of life and gather up those who are younger and afraid. We are called to charge forth into this world with the audacity that says, "Come, and let us do a fine thing for Jesus Christ!" *Oh, for a thousand tongues to sing our dear Redeemer's praise.* To join together in His army to confront the enemies of His Kingdom as citizens empowered, encouraged, and filled with the Holy Spirit.

W. E. Orchard wrote a prayer during WWI concerning crisis. He wrote so beautifully, *"Grant by Thy grace that we may not be found wanting in the hour of crisis. When the battle is set, may we know on which side we ought to be, and when the days go hard, cowards steal from the field, and heroes fall around the standard, may our place be found where the fight is the fiercest. If we faint, we may not be faithless; if we fall, may it be while facing the foe."*

Again, come, let you and I do a fine thing for Jesus Christ!

> *Father, grant me a willing spirit to go forth into this world with courage. May I never lose heart, but instead, may I stand firm upon your Word, speaking in boldness and in the power of Your Son, Jesus Christ. No matter my adversaries, no matter the trials, no matter the persecution, God, give to me a sound mind, integrity of heart and strength to be victorious in every circumstance. Amen.*

From Tongi to Karomtola

Ephesians 3:13-21

So I ask you not to lose heart over what I am suffering for you, which is your glory. For this reason I bow my knees Father, from whom every family in Heaven and on Earth is named, that according to the riches of His glory He may grant you to be strengthened with might through His Spirit in the inner man, and that Christ may dwell in your hearts through faith; that you, being routed and grounded in love, may have power to comprehend with all the saints what is the breadth and length and height and depth, and to know the love of Christ which surpasses knowledge, that you may be filled with all the fullness of God. Now to him who by the power at work within us is able to do far more abundantly than all that we ask or think, to him be glory in the church and in Christ Jesus to all generations, for ever and ever. Amen.

I have more fun than any Presbyterian minister I know; I get to work with some of the most unusual people in the whole world. They are your missionaries. They are men and women called by God to live in other countries with different cultures and languages who face things that would challenge many of us.

This summer Mickey and I were in Taiwan, Thailand, and Bangladesh. We had been spending a lot of time in Africa, but this summer we went to Thailand. We met the missionaries at a restaurant which was a favorite of theirs.

As we sit down at the table, the waiters come to take your order. At this restaurant in Thailand, you pick the cobra you want out of the cage and right at your table they tie its mouth shut, hang it, and clean it— all while it is alive. They drain the blood out, mix it with a little gin, and let you toss it back as a pick-me-up. I told them, "No thank you. I had mine at the hotel earlier in the day." That was amazing to watch.

Some people would be devastated by watching that ceremony. The missionaries take those sort of things in stride and go on about their day.

Some people have no business being in difficult situations like that. I will not say his name because, if I did, Tom Stewart, one of my colleagues, would be embarrassed to death.

Tom is a foot taller than I am and there is fifty pounds more of Tom. He is a big person with a big heart. It was 120 degrees in the shade in Bangladesh this time of the year. If it is not raining, steam is rising from the mud. It is a difficult place to be. Tom was dying in the heat.

When he gets to the guest house where we stay, he climbed all the way up seven stories in the heat to get to his room. As you can imagine, he is about to die to take a shower. He has been on the plane for about three days to get there. As he climbs into the shower, a little trickle of water is come out. He managed to soap up his huge body and the water stopped. Tom stood there dripping with water.

After drying, he goes down to dinner. Now try to imagine—they have put on their very best for my dear friend. It is a big table filled with missionaries from all over Bangladesh who have come to share in dinner and to meet Tom who has come all the way from the United States. Being polite, they ask Tom to say the blessing. My dear friend prayed with these dear people and said, "Oh dear Lord, get me out of Bangladesh."

Things have never been the same in that part of the world again!!

Our missionaries serve in difficult circumstances around the world. When I think of our missionaries, I think of Paul. Do you remember where Paul was when he wrote this letter? He was in prison. Paul was always in prison somewhere. It is one of the great things about him.

He is trapped in prison, probably chained to the wall. It is cold and nasty. It is beyond our imagination. It is a horrible experience. It would be defeating to most of us. You are simply overwhelmed. And look at what Paul says,

> *"Don't worry about me. Don't lose heart over me. I am praying for you. I bow my knees before the Father, that according to His riches in Glory, He may grant you to be strengthened, that you will know the power of Jesus Christ, that you will*

> know the height, the depth, the length, the breadth, the love of Christ which surpasses knowledge."

Do you hear the enthusiasm when he sang? Keep going. Paul is in prison. He is suffering horribly and yet he can say,

> "To him who by the power at work within us, is able to do more than any of us ever imagined. To him be all the glory, now and forever. Amen."

Now think about the reality of this situation. If you really take this seriously, you have to think in your mind, "Is Paul still with us? Is Paul kind of lost?" I mean think about this. This man is locked up in a horrible prison setting, and he is writing all these joyful words. And some of you are thinking inside, "You know, Ben, no big deal. Paul can write this. I mean, Paul is just in prison. Paul has just been tortured has to eat horrible food and live in terrible conditions. He can write joyful things like that, Ben. Paul could write that, Ben, but I couldn't write that."

"You want to talk about suffering. You have no idea what suffering is like. You ought to know my wife."

"I'll tell you about suffering. You ought to know my husband, Ben. Paul is not suffering. He does not have to live with the man I have to live with."

"Paul wasn't 83 years old when he wrote that, Ben. He does not know what it is like to be old. I can tell you about suffering."

The French invented the guillotine and the Exocet missile. There is also a device the French which is part of this next story.

We have huge megastores in the United States. One of these megastores is called American Fair. To get a shopping cart, you have to put a quarter in this machine which the French invented. Theoretically, it releases a shopping cart so one can shop. When one is finished shopping, the cart is brought back, reconnected, and the quarter is refunded.

Have you ever seen anything like this? No? They will get here soon. You undo the thing, it falls down and inevitably gets tangled with the cart in front, and it gets stuck. It is a very frustrating experience.

I have to confess. One day I lost my patience. I dutifully put in my quarter, disconnected the car and nothing happened. I pulled again and nothing happened. I sat there and discussed this with the shopping cart for a few minutes. Finally, I had it!

I tugged as hard as I could and out came eight shopping carts connected to each other. I decided I had been blessed, so I pushed all eight carts into the store. I went past checkout, and the clerk's eyes got big. She said, "What are you doing?" I said, "I am just going to pick up a few things. I'll be right back," as I kept pushing all eight shopping carts.

It is amazing how quickly I was surrounded by people who wanted to help me. They took the carts apart, and I had one little cart. The moral of the story? When enough noise is made, somebody is going to hear you and do something about it.

Bangladesh was formerly called East Pakistan. They had a war for independence. When they finished that horrible war, they were free, but they were dying. The little country of Bangladesh was strong enough to make enough noise for your missionary, Dr. Herb Coddington, to hear them all the way around into Korea.

Herb Coddington left Korea and went to Bangladesh before it was popular to be in Bangladesh. He was there before any of the relief agencies. Through Herb, you were the first ones there. He confronted the impossible. What he did was undoubtedly through power of Christ.

I would love to consistently feel like God can do abundantly more than I ever asked in need. I would love to feel like I am growing spiritually. Wouldn't you like to feel that? But in all of our lives there are things that get in the way of that. Herb confronted a situation with grace and glory which is a great example of how we can live our daily lives.

The people of Bangladesh believed that after the war they would be swamped with tourists. They had beautiful posters made that read, "Discover Bangladesh before the tourist do."

In preparation for this influx of tourism, the government of Bangladesh sent army trucks into the capital of Dhaka. They turned over the garbage cans, locked up the drainage ditches, rounded up 44,000 of the poorest people, and relocated those folks 15 miles out of town in a fenced field called Tongi. The entire area was less than one square mile for 44,000 people. There was no food and no water. There was no sanitation, no housing, and no medical care. And it was to that impossible situation that your missionary, Herb Coddington, arrived and stood as your baptismal font faces you. He stood before a fence at a refugee camp and stared into the blank eyes of 44,000 people.

Herb must have thought, "Please, Lord, Get me out of Bangladesh." I am sure that the prospect of trying to stop the starvation, save the dying, and give comfort was more than anybody could begin to fathom.

I imagine Herb must have said as he stared at this sea of eyes, "to him who is able to do, far more abundantly than we dare to ask." He must have claimed that verse for himself as he faced the crowd and went on with the day.

Everyone was suffering from malnutrition. Some were starving, while others were dying of thirst. Those who were alive had parasites. Tuberculosis, a disgustingly awful and unnecessary disease, was epidemic in the camp. There was no family planning, and the water was dirty and infested with disease.

He began with the immediate problems: water, food and shelter. They dug wells and clean water was found 25 feet down. The mothers got it in their jars, gave it to their babies, and called it, "living water" because when they gave it to their babies, their babies lived.

Next, he put a rope down the middle of the camp as if down the middle of your sanctuary. People on one side were fed one day and the people on the other side of the rope were the next day.

Imagine a little boy who has a piece of bread sitting on the ground next to the rope giving half of his bread to a stranger on the other side.

When missionaries come and speak to you, we don't want half of what you've got, but we want a piece of it. Remember that. It doesn't take much to change the world, but it takes something. Without it, we can't do it. Herb began by feeding people every other day.

Next, he began to treat the diseases. He triaged people with tuberculosis and treated them first. Then, he treated neonatal tetanus. This disease is contracted when baby is born on a mud floor, a rusty knife cuts the umbilical cord, and animal manure is rubbed on the baby's belly. The baby gets tetanus or lockjaw and dies. The mortality rate for these children was extremely high. One at a time, he treated all the unnecessary suffering in the camp.

At the same time, he began to teach them how to have sanitary water. He taught the mothers to she would boil the water before the baby drank it, and, the baby will be okay. Clean water takes care of the parasites, too. By simply boiling the water, 75 percent of the diseases would be eradicated.

As I saw and heard what he had done, I began to think, "You know that makes so much sense, doesn't it?" And I know that in my Christian life, there are times when the things that make good old fashion common sense are the things that I generally ignore. I hear the words of Scripture and there are words that are so filled with the grandeur of it all, that I am convinced those words will not apply to me. They might apply to Dan or the elders in the church. They might apply to those people who exude Jesus Christ, but they do not apply to me. They do not because times are tough over here in this part of my life. Or I am spending so much time worried about the war, the economy and the recession or my age, and my relationships at home. When I hear words about the abundant power of Christ, I wonder if it applies to me.

Just as Herb Coddington faced an absolutely hopeless situation, and gave it to the Lord, I think today we can take what he did, and apply it to our lives. I think we, too, can see miracles just as we have seen in Tongi.

It is very simple.

First, make a list. Write two words "survey" and "honest." If Herb Coddington had looked at that refugee camp and said, "Well there are 44,000 people here and they really look pretty good, they would have died. He looked at them and said, "*Honestly,* these are the problems...there is no food and no water. There is tuberculosis and parasites. On your sheet of paper, write down those things which have compromised your life. Write down where your soul is hungry. Write down the parasites that chip away at the relationships of your life.

Am I Ever Going to Get Out of Here?

Write down the things that get in the way of your attitude about living.

Second, prioritize the list. Well, how do I pick? I make this long list of all the things that are good and all the things that need attention. How do I choose? Listen, it is very simple. Let me tell you where to start.

1. If you are doing something that is killing you, stop it. That is simple enough. Look at your list. If you are still smoking, stop it. That is going to kill you.
2. If you are doing something to yourself spiritually that is ruining your relationship with Jesus Christ, stop it.

That is where you start. Do a survey and prioritize things that must be dealt with.

Third, address each problem. That's why God has given each of us who are the personification of grace and love. They are there to say, "I'll never judge you, but I'll stand with you." That is why there is such a thing as confession. Maybe that is where it needs to start. And I am going to tell you the most difficult one first of all.

Men, maybe you need to sit down with her and pour your heart out to her. This time I want to assure you that she is not going to say anything smart aleck back. This time she is not going to make fun of you. This time she is going to listen and not throw something back at you. Because this time she is listening also to the word. She wants to see you take a step together.

If it has to start with confession, do it. If you have to pick up the phone and call that person, call them today and confess it. If you need to repair a relationship, do it now. That is one of the things standing in the way of the joy that Paul felt. That is one of the things that lets you out of the prison that holds us. Do an honest survey. Set your priorities with life threatening things and begin to address each.

Fourth, learn where to get help. Perhaps you are sitting here thinking, "I'd love to know what this is all about. But if I showed up at a Bible study, somebody would say, "What are 'you' doing here?"

I want to promise you something else. On the back of your bulletin, there are more Bible studies than you could ever imagine. Let me speak for everyone in this church and say, "If you'll just come, all you will meet are people who are thrilled that you are here because we are not walking to leave folks behind. We are walking together through this life. And we are learning together."

And the last step is so simple: prevention. In the refugee camp that meant educating, drilling wells, teaching others to teach others. It also means prayer. Beside the word prevent, write the word prayer. Surround yourself by that power. Well, what happened at the refugee camp? You noticed the sermon title. It looks like a Bob Hope movie doesn't it? "From Tongi to Karomtola." Isn't that great?

You don't have to do that now, but sometime try saying that right out loud. It is more fun. Doesn't it sound like a Bob Hope movie? You can just see him in a jeep going over the mountains on the road to Karomtola. Let me tell you another story.

When Mickey and I were there, I stood there with tears running down my face. Mickey took a little harp and started playing, and before you knew it, we were surrounded by thousands. They were all big and fat.

There is no more malnutrition there because of you. A baby has not died of neonatal tetanus in three years because of you. Ninety percent of those children have been immunized against polio because of you. Sixty percent of those families practice family planning because of you. Right now, forty percent of our patients are coming from outside the refugee camp to be with you.

You have done such a miracle that you are packing your bags and your moving from Tongi to a terrible place called Karomtola. Why? Because where do you expect to find your missionaries but in the most difficult places in the world. And praise God, people who have a vision, are going to do it all again.

Wherever you are right now in your life, whatever is waiting for you out here, no matter how you feel in prison, perhaps you feel like a refugee yourself, I hold out to you this day, just as Paul held out to his friends in Ephesus, that because of Jesus Christ and His Church, each of us is free to claim the love, forgiveness, mercy, and grace of the one who is at work within us who is able to do far more abundantly than all that we ask or think. And to Him, be glory in the church in Christ Jesus to all generations, forever and ever. Amen.

How Then Shall We Live?

"And Jesus went about all the cities and villages, teaching in their synagogues and preaching the gospel of the kingdom, and healing every disease and every infirmity. When he saw the crowds, he had compassion for them, because they were harassed and helpless, like sheep without a shepherd. Then he said to his disciples, 'The harvest is plentiful, but the laborers are few; pray therefore the Lord of the harvest to send out laborers into his harvest.'" Matthew 9:35-38 (RSV)

I believe God calls us to specific ministries. I am a Presbyterian minister, and my call is to serve the medical mission work of the Presbyterian Church around the world.

Presbyterians currently operate mission hospitals in 80 locations around the world. Presbyterians also operate over 120 nursing and medical technology schools, as well as several thousand rural and jungle public health clinics and rally posts. The goal in each location is the same: *We are to heal often, cure sometimes, but always show the compassion of Jesus Christ.*

My ministry includes traveling to remote locations and learning of the work of our missionaries. I spend the majority of my time traveling for my church and promoting this wonderful ministry. It is an exciting life, but it raises for me a constant question. When I see how the rest of the world has to live, and then I see how we as Americans get to live, the question is obvious, "How then shall we live?"

Thank goodness God's Word is clear and specific. As we begin, let me ask you to do two things: I would like you to re-read the text from Mathew 9. As you read the words, underline the words that catch your attention. In addition, as you read, ask a specific request of the Lord. "Father, do not inspire us, do not give us history; give us answers. We want to learn from your word how you would have us live as American Christians in these days." With that assignment before you, go back and read the passage; and then we will continue.

Which words caught your eye? For many, the answer is teaching, preaching and healing. For others, the words compassion, laborers or harvest catches an eye. As I read the passage for the first time, I saw the words "harassed and helpless." Jesus saw the crowds in His world, and they accurately fit that description.

Harassed is much more than one child picking on another child. It is actually a word that is used to describe a body or a corpse that has been mangled and torn to pieces. It is descriptive of one whose world is destroyed around them, as if in a war.

Helpless is much more than an infant who cannot fend for itself. It is actually a violent word. Helpless describes someone who has been up, punched in the face and knocked off their feet. With those poignant descriptions, our Lord saw the people around Him.

As I travel the world, my conclusion is obvious. Those same people who were harassed and helpless in Jesus' day are still with us, there are simply more of them.

As believers in Christ, we are called to respond to their presence. I have been privileged to see how the governments of the world respond to suffering. In one location, a school was built, complete with an in-ground swimming pool. The school cost over $1,000,000 U.S. and seven years later, it was still empty. The school was never needed in the first place, but an attempt was made to meet a need, before a need was ascertained.

In another location, a 250-bed hospital was constructed. Tragically, and in the fervor of development, someone forgot to add plumbing to the building and currently, the jungle is reclaiming this hospital as merely dust. It is apparent to me that if the governments of the world were capable of solving the problems before us, they would have accomplished it long ago.

Jesus saw the crowds, and He did not build a building. He did not write a check, and He certainly did not appoint a task force to create a study paper and have a luncheon somewhere. Jesus saw the crowds, and according to our text, He had compassion for them.

Compassion is a beautiful word, it describes the emotion we feel when we come upon someone suffering, but there is a key word in the definition. The key word is unnecessarily, suffering unnecessarily. In this world, if you are hungry and cannot get something to eat, you are suffering unnecessarily. If you are sick and cannot receive adequate medical care, you are suffering unnecessarily. Whether you live in Mbuji Mayi, Zaire, or Minneapolis, Minnesota, if you are living with anything less than a vital, vibrant, and alive relationship with Jesus Christ, then whether you know it or not you are suffering, and suffering unnecessarily!

Let me describe the compassion of the Church of Jesus Christ. I make the rounds to every ward of our hospitals around the world. I stay amazed at the tender caring of our nurses, physicians, and chaplaincy staff around the world. It is obvious to me that the surgeon's knife and the nurse's touch go hand in hand with the Word and sacrament. As I make my rounds, I always visit the pediatric wards last of all. So often, the children in pediatric wards are suffering from some form of advanced malnutrition, or some other deadly disease. So often the best we can offer is the tender loving compassion of Jesus Christ to the blessed children who die so needlessly around the world.

On one particular occasion, I was visiting the Good Shepherd Hospital in Zaire. I had been to every ward where I attempted to communicate with every patient in every bed. While I speak a little bit of a lot of languages, I find that one can communicate the love of Christ through a touch, a smile, a stroke of the hair or a pat on the back. I can pray in any language and the Lord will receive it. I had been to every ward, and now it was time to visit the children's area.

I entered the small isolation room as quietly as possible. One chair and one small bed comprised the furniture in this dark green room. The curtains were drawn on the single window and the shutters were placed in such a way that the room appeared darker than mid-day. An exhausted mother sat in the chair beside the baby's bed. She barely lifted her head to look at me as I walked into the room.

In the middle of the small bed was a little boy. He was too weak to make a sound and too weak to lift his arms. His white hair, wrinkled skin and lethargic attitude belied the fact that this child was two years old. He was no longer than a gallon bucket and he weighed less than 10 pounds.

I took his picture, put my camera down, and picked the little boy up in my arms. As I held this child, he died. His physical body was simply too weak to continue fighting the effects of malnutrition. His mother cried as any mother would cry. Parents around the world love their children as dearly as we in the United States love our own. The nurses came into the room and allowed the mother a few moments to hold her child. In traditional Zairian form, she left the hospital room following a cart with her sheet draped little boy.

As the cart was wheeled out of the room, she cried at the top of her lungs. She spoke in her own language about her little boy. She talked of the joy he had given to her life. She talked of the joy of watching him play. She talked of his gentle spirit. She cried to God for mercy.

I returned to my room in the guesthouse and sat on the edge of the bed crying. I felt that day a feeling I have known too many other times since. This boy was the first child to die in my arms. Tragically, he was not the last. I felt fat and nauseated. I felt angry at God and wanted to cry out, "Oh Lord, why did that little boy have to die? What did he ever do wrong? Why not me, Lord? I have seen it all, and I have done it all, why not me?"

As I experienced the valley of the shadow of death, I heard someone singing outside my window. I brushed the tears from my eyes and thought to myself, "Oh great, here comes company. This is not what I need right now." I pulled back the curtains and looked across my front yard and saw her skipping and dancing. She appeared to be the size of a five-year-old. She was bald headed.

Malnourished black children often experience a change in hair and skin color due to protein deficiency. Their black curly hair generally turns red, gray or varying shades of white. Uneducated parents occasionally change in hair color is the cause of death, so they shave the baby's head so it will not die.

This little girl was bald headed. With no shoes, she wore the white rags of a little dress. She was skipping and singing at the top of her lungs, "E twaku sanka bwa luce lua Jesu." Translated into English, those beautiful words represent the Zairian version of the children's song, "Jesus Loves Me."

The translation is not a direct one to English, but says instead, "Yes we were happy, when Jesus came into our lives." As I watched the little girl, it dawned on me that she was one of the children from the nutrition center at the Good Shepherd Hospital.

Do you know what the compassion of Jesus Christ is? The compassion of Jesus Christ is the stuff that filled her little belly with food and it's the stuff that filled her heart with the knowledge of Jesus Christ. Combining those two ingredients enabled her to skip along and sing, and my first thought was, "A little child shall lead them." No, we did not get to that little boy in time. He died in my arms. He did not need to die, but he did; however, we got to that little girl in time. She was going to be fine. She represented hope for me, and I regained the strength to get up and face it all again.

Halfway around the world, Dr. David Seel, Medical Director of the Presbyterian Medical Center of Chonju, Korea, wrote about the compassion of Christ. David writes, "Every man, woman and child who comes before me, bears the image of God's life-giving spirit. Jesus went farther than when He said, 'What you do unto the least of these you do also unto Me.' I cannot possibly remember that every face in the long parade is Christ, as exemplified in my patient."

David raises some difficult issues with this quote. It calls us to question how we live. It calls us to question the way we treat the people who sit in the pews next to us in church, around our breakfast tables, in the pictures and stories from third world countries; it causes us to question the way we treat the face in the mirror.

Do we have the courage to remember that every one of those faces deserves the respect, the love, and the compassion that we would show to Jesus Christ himself? That is not easy. To learn more, let us address the second assignment given to you at the beginning of this chapter.

At the beginning of this chapter, I asked you to read the Scripture looking for specific answers. Remember this for your own Bible study. As you read the Word of God, always ask yourself, "What is Jesus doing, saying, being or transforming that serves as an example for me?" Combining that with an accurate word study will enable God's Word to come more to life for you.

Jesus traveled about teaching, preaching, and healing. In one word, what is He doing that speaks to us about life in these days? Some of you may want to answer that Jesus is doing "ministry." That is true. However, if you are a layman in the Church, and I pushed you on this issue, you would say that is what clergy are supposed to do. That is true and that also lets you off the hook. The Word of God never lets any of us off the hook!

If I pushed you again, some of you might pick up on the word traveling. To that end, you would want to describe Jesus as a missionary. That is true. Some of you would go further than that and say to yourselves, "Ben wants me to say, 'If I want to know how to live, I should be a missionary.'" That is true also. However, if I pushed a little harder, you would probably tell me that your church already supports missionaries, and that is their job and that lets you off the hook again! I am sorry, but I must repeat myself, "God's Word never lets us off the hook!"

Let us boil it down a little bit more. Jesus is traveling. Jesus is teaching. Jesus is preaching. Jesus is healing. Why did the Father send the Son? Did the Father not send the Son to preach, teach and heal, that all the world would be reconciled unto Himself? Of course He did! Then it only follows, if Jesus is doing what the Father sent Him to do, then Jesus is simply being obedient! If we look at our lives as disciples of Jesus Christ, aren't we called first of all, to be obedient to the will of God for our lives? Of course we are! What does that mean?

I believe that spiritual self-examination begins in **solitude.** In a world that is so filled with distraction, it is important to go to a quiet place to pray. This is a scriptural mandate set by the example of our Lord.

Find a quiet place. Place before the Lord the fabric of your life and examine it. Ask of God some basic questions, "Father, here is the fabric of my life. There are some stains over here. There are some worn spots over here. On this side there are even some tattered, frayed edges. Father, here is the fabric of my life. Am I living it in obedience to your will for me?"

If you can find that you are living your life in obedience to Jesus Christ, then rejoice and tell someone about it because you have learned something about sacrifice.

If there is a common denominator in an effective Christian's life, it is **sacrifice.** Let me use the mission field as an example.

Am I Ever Going to Get Out of Here?

The servants of our Lord who give their lives in developing nations, live a life of daily sacrifice. They have sacrificed their own desires for material wealth, comfort and security, for a life on the razor's edge. Developing nations offer little in the way of comfort and accommodation. A steady diet of rice, beans and boiled water can take a toll on anyone's existence. Only by removing self as the center of our being and allowing our lives to be filled with the presence of Christ, can we truly live a sacrificial Christian life.

This process is not easy, and it is probably best described as the culmination of sanctification. How then shall we live, but obediently unto sacrifice? You recall our discussion concerning compassion. That is a beautiful word with a particularly moving definition. I especially like the use of the word "unnecessary" suffering. That is the key. Compassion is a beautiful word, but compassion by itself accomplishes nothing. I want to give you a test and I want you to be honest with yourself. Here we go.

> (a) Have you ever watched one of the many television programs concerning the suffering in Ethiopia, India, or another tragic part of the world?
>
> (b) Did that program upset you?
>
> (c) Did any of you actually shed a tear, or feel a lump in your throat because of the graphic depiction of suffering?

> (d) If you have seen such a program and were moved to compassion, why is it then, that most of you did absolutely nothing about it?

The answer is simple. Compassion by itself does nothing. Consider for a moment the disciples in the John 9. They came upon the blind man and in their compassion wanted to know who sinned since this man was born blind. In their compassion, they were more worried about whose fault it was than what could be done about it! Out of his obedience, Jesus responded, "It was not that this man or his parents sinned. It is show that the works of God might be made manifest in him." Then Jesus gave that man his sight!

You see, Jesus had an understanding of life which is ours to gain as well. Out of His obedience, Jesus understood an old saying, "Man's extremity is God's opportunity." Consider it for a moment. When you are at either end of life is when the Lord has His best chance to deal with you. Do you remember graduating from school? Do you remember asking her to marry you? Do you remember your husband asking you to marry him? Do you remember getting that first job or that significant promotion? Do you remember when that baby was born and everyone was all right? Whenever something wonderful happens to us it lifts us so high and we all want to proclaim, "Praise the Lord!"

On the other hand, if we flunk out of school, if we lose a job, if our marriage fails, if a baby is born and everything is not all right—when we are the ones who are harassed and helpless—what happens? I do not know about you, but I land on my knees. I cry to the Lord, "Oh, Lord, please get me through just one more day."

When we are at either extreme in life, the Lord has his best chance to reach out and grab us. He looked at the crowds of people who were harassed and helpless, and out of His obedience, He was optimistic! He looked at the crowds and said, "The harvest is plentiful!" The hungry people of the world really want something to eat—we can feed them! The sick people of the world really want to feel better—we can accomplish that! The people whose lives are lost and lonely—we have something for them; it is called the Good News of the Gospel!

Out of His obedience, the Lord was optimistic—for there is so much that even we can do! How then shall we live? Obediently unto sacrifice, and optimistically unto foolishness. We have before us the wonderful optimism of Jesus Christ. With His optimism, how can we ever fail?

He was optimistic, but he was also realistic. He said, "The harvest is plentiful, but laborers are few." Let me tell you what a laborer for Jesus Christ is by telling you what it is not.

I was raised in Memphis, Tennessee. When I turned 17, I had the job opportunity of a lifetime. I got to leave my home in Memphis, and spend a summer digging ditches for a construction company in Florida. We were building a hotel in St. Petersburg, Florida.

Imagine the scenario. There was literally a huge field of white, broiling sand. The summer sun relentlessly beat down upon us It was hot and difficult. Just the sort of work that a young 17-year-old loves!

Each day, I spent seven hours in a long line of men digging ditches in the sand. The man next to me had just gotten off the boat from Cuba. He spoke no English and to this day, the only Spanish I can speak includes, nacho, taco, guacamole, and refried beans!

Each day, at about 2:30 in the afternoon, this man put his shovel down, looked at me and said a word that sounded like "econdiendotay." I know that word is not a Spanish word; however phonetically, that is what it sounded like to me. I responded, "Well, I am doing pretty well today, how about yourself?" He responded with a puzzled expression as he put his shovel down and disappeared for a while.

Some time passed before it dawned on me that he wanted me to go with him. He put his shovel down, tugged on my shoulder, and said, "Econdiendotay." I put my shovel down and responded, "Okay, I am going your way."

We walked around to the backside of the building, where there was small opening which led to a crawlspace. We got on our hands and knees and crawled under the building.

I learned several things at that time. I learned that the crawlspace is where all the pipes and plumbing belong and it was dark. It is about 30 degrees cooler there and the foreman was not in the crawlspace! We went to the backside of the building, settled down in the sand, and relaxed. I figured out right that "econdiendotay" meant, "Let's go hide." From that day on, we "econdiendotayed" about once or twice a day!

Now that is a delightful story, but I also believe that it points to a basic truth: The Lord never calls us to look at the difficulties of life and respond by putting down our shovels to hide in a crawl space. Instead, He calls us to obediently and optimistically labor in His harvest.

Let us respond to the mandate of our Lord,

> *"Pray therefore, the Lord of the harvest to send out laborers into His harvest."*

Jesus makes it very clear that we are to implore the Father to raise up men and women to serve on the mission fields of the Church.

My best hope is that you will join with me in praying for two people. First of all, pray specifically for someone in your own congregation. You do not need to know much about that person because we know much about Jesus Christ. I want you to pray that no matter who that person happens to be that the Lord will grant to them a new hunger and thirst for obedience to His will. I want you to pray that the Lord will reach within their hearts and turn up a bright flame of optimism about all of life—for there is so much we can do!

In addition, I want you to pray that same prayer for yourself. As you do, bear in mind that the Lord hears and responds to our prayers. If you ask the Lord to show you a new way to serve, please be prepared obediently and optimistically to respond.

> *Heavenly Father, I ask that you break my heart for the things of this world that breaks yours. Help me to no longer be apathetic to the suffering and misery that I witness in this fallen world. Give to me a compassion that not only stirs my heart, but compels me to act as you would act. Equip me to use the gifts that you have given to me to alleviate the hurt in people's lives, to shine forth light into their darkness and to model mercy as you demonstrated when you were on earth. May I follow after you, Jesus, and go forth and teach, preach and heal wherever you may lead.*

How to Survive in this World

Joshua 1:7-9

"Be strong and very courageous. Be careful to obey all the law my servant Moses gave you; do not turn from it to the right or to the left, that you may be successful wherever you go. Do not let this Book of the Law depart from your mouth; meditate on it day and night, so that you may be careful to do everything written in it. Then you will be prosperous and successful. Have I not commanded you? Be strong and courageous. Do not be terrified; do not be discouraged, for the Lord your God will be with you wherever you go." (NIV)

I have friends who live in a place called Suncheon, South Korea. They are all blind. They are horribly maimed and disfigured because of leprosy. Leprosy is curable today, but when these folks got it, it wasn't curable.

Leprosy attacks the ends of things. The nerves at the ends of fingers. The nerves at the end of the optic nerve. That's why in later stages sight is lost. These folks really do not look human, and they realized early on that if they did not bury God's Word in their heart, a very difficult life would become an impossible life. It took them 25 years to do this. They memorized the entire Bible.

Think about that. I cannot remember my license plate number! I don't know any of my PINs (Personal Identification Numbers). What I do know is that I have to bury God's Word in my heart or life is going to be tougher than it ever needs to be. So this morning, I am going to teach you a passage of Scripture, so by the time we leave here today, you will carry it in your heart like I carry it in mine.

It is from 1st Corinthians 16. Listen to the Word of God:

> *"Keep alert, stand firm in your faith, be courageous, be strong. Let all that you do be done in love."* (NRSV)

Paul wrote these words in the Letter to the Corinthians. Paul's job in the early church was to travel around the known world, tell people about Jesus, plant a church, and then move on and do it again at another location.

Paul went to Corinth. He told people about Jesus, and he started a church. He headed on down the road, and somewhere in his travels people caught up with Paul and they said, "Paul, we have problems in Corinth." There was another group of people who were trying to form a church, and they couldn't stand each other!

They argued about everything! They argued about who was God and who was not God. They argued about what one could eat and what one could not eat. They had moral issues. They had more problems than you could ever imagine, so Paul wrote a letter to try to get these folks back on track.

Have you ever been part of a group that did not get along? Perhaps your family doesn't get along. Maybe your civic organization has a small group which wants to control the

Am I Ever Going to Get Out of Here?

entire group. It is awful, isn't it? It's a terrible experience. We always end up with an "us" and a "them." If it's really bad, there is an "us" and a "them" and a "them" and a "them" and a "them" and on it goes.

Well, let's think about Corinth for a minute. Who was right? There were two groups in the church which could not stand each other. Paul wrote a letter to the church to address the conflict.

Paul admonishes them to "keep alert," "stand firm in your faith," and "be courageous and be strong!" Each group thought Paul meant these words only for them, and it only entrenched the division—both groups believed they were right! "Let everything you do be done in love." Now, if you're not from the South, you don't know this. In the South, this is what we call a bless-your-heart passage." Everybody in the South knows I can say anything about anyone I want as long as I preface it with, "Bless your heart." "You know, you're not the brightest light on the Christmas tree, but you're one of the ornaments. Bless your heart!"

My wife, Mickie, and I moved to Dawsonville, Georgia. Mickie is a college professor at Brenau University. She is from Japan. My son, Adam, is in Iraq for his third tour. I went to Iraq and was embedded with my son's company of Marines. At the same time, Mickie decided she wanted to fight terrorism.

You'd have to know Mickie to completely understand this story. Mickie became a United States citizen so she could apply for a Fulbright Scholarship to be a visiting professor in the Middle East. This gave her an opportunity to teach Islamic women and serve them as her way to fight terrorism. She spent a year at the University of Doha in Qatar.

When we moved to our house, we decided to have a dinner party for our new neighbors. Upstairs on the porch, there is big dining table. I sat at one end of the table, and Mickie sat beside me. At the other end of the table was a woman I did not know.

When we were about five minutes into the conversation, I discovered that this lady and I were at opposite ends of the spectrum on EVERYTHING! We proceeded to have an argument of the ugly kind. I stood up, and she stood up, and she and her husband abruptly went home.

The next morning, I wrote this lady a letter. I had to do something...it was just terrible. So I wrote her a letter which said:

> Dear Jane,
>
> It was great to meet you last night. I'm so glad that we live here. I am thrilled you are my neighbor. I think it's wonderful that we don't always have to agree on everything, but bless your heart, you're wrong and you're going to the devil.
>
> Love, Ben.

I put that in her mailbox, and she called me on the phone, and she said, "Ben, it was so nice to meet you. It was so much fun being able to carry on a conversation with you. I so appreciate your letter and I want you to know I took your letter and I framed it." I said, "You did?" She said, "Yeah, I hung it in the bathroom."

I want to present something to you that's radical; Paul made a mistake. Scripture says, "Keep alert. Stand firm in your faith. Be courageous, be strong, and let everything you do be done in love." Paul didn't mean to say that. Here's what happened.

Paul heard about the church in Corinth. He prays, "All right Lord, I've got to write them a letter. Tell me what to say."

While Paul is in the middle of writing this letter, he hears this KNOCK, KNOCK, and KNOCK. He looks around and then he goes back to writing when again he hears KNOCK, KNOCK, and KNOCK.

He looks up, and there is his dear, old, and wise friend, Theopholis. Theopholis is standing there with his sandals on, and he is tapping his sandal on the ground and Paul says, "Can I help you?"

Theopholis says, "You know Paul, the boat is going to leave in about 20 minutes. If you want me to get that letter to those folks, you had better step on it."

Paul says, "Okay, just give me a second." He's writing and writing and writing. He writes, "Keep alert, stand firm in your faith, be courageous, be strong, let everything you do be done in love."

He takes the letter, rolls it up, gives it to his friend, and his friend disappears into history. As soon as Theopholis is out the door, Paul thinks, "Hum, I didn't mean to say that. I didn't mean to say keep alert, stand firm in your faith, be courageous, be strong, and let everything you do be done in love." What I meant to say was, "Let everything you do be done in love. Keep alert for ways to love people in the name of Jesus."

You've seen all those silly bumper stickers that encourage us to, "Do Random Acts of Kindness." Instead, I proclaim that as a Christian, you are called to do intentional acts of compassion in the name of Christ. Being a Christian is the greatest excuse in the world for caring for strangers. We are to share what we have, to open doors for others, to show kindness in traffic and a multitude of other acts of compassion. If someone asks you why you did such an act, your reply would be easy, "I'm a believer in Jesus." Simply let it go at that.

My friends in Korea, whom I spoke of earlier, who memorized the Bible, have nothing. They don't even look human. A missionary told them about a need and in spite of their physical challenges, these precious people were keeping alert for a way to love. That same missionary got them harmonicas. They don't have fingers, but they still have the palms of what used to be hands and these folks discovered they could hold these harmonicas, and they formed a harmonica choir that is absolute amazing!

They travel around South Korea. They perform, and they raise money, and they give it all away! They give it all to children who are orphans on the streets of Seoul, South Korea. In their opinion, these children are worse off than they are.

My sermon title is, "How to Survive in this World." Let's throw that out and say instead, "How to Thrive in this World." Christian, if you want to know how to be overflowing with life, you need to keep alert for ways to love people in the name of Jesus Christ.

Next Sunday I will be in Kinshasa. We will go to church, eat lunch, and we will take a nap which is a standard routine around the world. One difference, however, is in the afternoons we will get in a truck and we will drive outside of town on a dirt road to a wall which is as high as the walls inside this church. The wall is painted white and written in huge letters—Spiritual Combat.

When we arrive, we grab a chair, and we'll walk to a gathering spot, an open air canopy-like structure. It has a big tin roof with no sides or no electricity. We sing, read Scripture, listen to sermons, and then we get on our knees in the sand and pray. Here's the fascinating part. Picture 10,000 Christians of all different backgrounds under this one roof.

When we start to pray, there are probably 40 languages represented and the best way to describe it is that it sounds like a thunderstorm. It rolls across that tin roof, and it goes down and then it comes back up in a big wave of people praying right out loud on their knees in the sand!

The first time I went I said, "Omba, what are we praying for?" He said to me, "For the first time in 45 years, our country has a chance to be free and we know that unless we fight the forces of darkness our country will not be free. We come here to pray the basics of our faith. We come here for spiritual combat."

I wonder what would happen in this country if we kept alert for ways to love. Furthermore, could you imagine if there was a way that we could bring thousands of Americans together weekly from all backgrounds, simply to pray for the basics that our country would be free!

I am so very proud of my sons, Ben and Adam. When Adam was on his third tour in the Middle East, he called me and said, "Hey dad. I've got a great idea. Why don't you come to Iraq?" I said, "Okay, I'm not doing anything."

I went to my radio network and before I knew it, I was in Iraq as a credentialed embedded journalist. I got to be with my son for a month on the front lines of that war in a place called Haditha, located in western Iraq. I got to sleep next to my kid and go on patrol with the Marines. I did everything that the Marines do and it was quite a life changing experience. It was really an amazing opportunity.

One of the things that the Marines do in that part of the world is to look for IEDs, or Improvised Explosive Device. When they are on patrol, they dig around in garbage cans, they kick over cardboard boxes, or they dig up piles of dirt in the middle of the road and hope it doesn't blow up.

Am I Ever Going to Get Out of Here?

We came back from one of those patrols and I maintained my agreement with the Marine Corps, which was that my son and I would keep protocol. I called my son, Lt. Mathes and he called me, Dr. Mathes.

We came in from patrol, and he walked up and said, "Dr. Mathes, can I visit with you a moment sir?" I said, "Absolutely sir." He took me into this room and he shut the door and I knew I was in trouble because he turned around and said, "Dad."

He told me, "My Marines tell me you were out on patrol. Is this true?" I said, "Yeah, I was out on patrol." He said, "My Marines tell me they were looking for IEDs: Digging around in garbage cans, kicking over boxes and stuff. Is that true?" I said, "Yes, that's true." Adam got real serious looking and he said, "Dad, my Marines told me that you were digging around in the garbage cans, kicking over cardboard boxes, and that you were down there digging up mounds of dirt in the road. Were you doing that?" I said, "Well, my understanding is that I can do whatever they do. If they're going to do that, I'm going to do that too because we are on patrol together." My son said, "Now, Dad, you know, when you get a compliment from your kid, it carries you a long way." My son looked at me like a first lieutenant does and said, "Courageous" and walked out the door and went back to war.

When I got back so many people said, "Were you ever afraid when you were on patrol in Iraq?" The answer is really simple, "When you are in the palm of the Lord's hand and you are surrounded by the United States Marines, there isn't anything to be afraid of."

I am no longer with the Marines, but I'm still in the palm of the Lord's hand, and this is what I know. I know that there are people in this place who are scared. You might be scared about what's going to happen to our country. You might be worried about your job. It may not be there tomorrow and you know that. Things at home may not be nearly as pretty as you look right now and you're scared. There may be some of you who are by yourself for the first time, and that's scary because you've confused being by yourself with being alone.

Christian, let me tell you something, if you don't hear anything else. You are NEVER alone. You may be by yourself, but you are NEVER alone.

What I have learned in my life is that I am in the palm of the Lord's hand, but when I need strength, I surround myself with Christians of great courage because that courage is contagious.

The scripture says "be strong." The Bible doesn't really say be strong. It really says to strengthen and to grow stronger. The apostle Paul knew that if we keep alert for ways to love, if we stand firm in our faith, and if we are courageous, then we will grow stronger in our faith. Isn't that right?

And then everything we do will be done in love. You already do everything out of love. The question is, "Love of what?" Is everything you do out of love of controlling your family? Is everything you do out of love of "looking good?" Are you more worried about your fat or your faith? Which one is it? Is everything you do out of love of money? What do you worry about more, cash or Christ?

I met a guy in Brazil. Rimaldo wanted it all and was going to do it all out of love, but it was love of power, money, and control. Rimaldo figured out the best way to get money, power, and control was to become the drug dealer in Codija, Brazil. He was great. He kept alert. He stood firm in what he believed. He was courageous. He was strong and he did it out of love for money, power, and control.

Rimaldo bought a piece of land. He built a house on the piece of land. You could go to the house and buy your drugs. You could use your drugs right there. It was one-stop shopping. This man had it all until he met the overwhelming love of God in Jesus Christ. It knocked this man to his knees. He left Codija, Brazil. Four years later he returned traveling from Manaus, Brazil. Rimaldo traveled down the Amazon River to Codija, Brazil, and got off the boat, but this time he got off the boat, not as a drug dealer but as a Presbyterian minister.

Rimaldo moved back into the drug house and began tearing it down, one board at a time, symbolically one board at a time, tearing down this drug house. In its place we are building a Presbyterian church on the same piece of property where you once could do drugs. New lives in Christ are going to be born.

Let me tell you something. There isn't a life in this church that is as messed up as Rimaldo's life used to be. You may want to sit and pour your heart out to one of us and just tell us a horrible story. I'm sorry, Rimaldo can top it. This man was downright evil.

What I know is, if God in Jesus Christ can take that life and completely transform it, do you hear the hope that this represents for you? Do you hear that? If God can transform Rimaldo's life, then you, then me, then we, then all of us can have a life that is filled with hope, courage, strength, and the love of God in Jesus Christ.

The problem is some folks don't want to believe that. That is just a lot of talk. I've got an answer for that. Our God loves you so much that he realizes that we have to have more than talk. We have to taste, we have to touch, and we have to feel His love. So our God gives us what we call a visible sign of His invisible grace. It's right here before me. It's the body and blood of our Lord who said to all Christians of all backgrounds, "If you are a believer in Christ, this table is for you." If today is the day that you need to covenant afresh with the Lord, if this is the day you've finally decided to stop it, it's killing you or if this is the day that you've finally decided to get over it, then join us at this table. If today is the day that you decide to forget about that past hurt because it was a long time ago, if this is the day that you decide to take a step, to pick it up, to put it down, to write a check, to call him and say put me to work, or to accept that the Lord has called you, then I don't know a better day than right now to join us at this table and join us in the celebration and the sacrament of the Lord's Supper.

If you are a believer in Christ, this is your table. This is our celebration as we remember together, the grace, the hope, the sacrifice, and the presence of the Lord in our lives. God bless you. Stay strong and God Bless America.

> *Jesus, you know those who have recommitted their lives to you today, those who have finally had enough of the struggles in their lives, those who made the decision today to exchange fear for faith, and you know too those who are still bound by their sins, their fears and even their pride. For all those here today I ask that you impart a measure of courage, strength and increase their faith. May many leave here today have changed from the inside out, filled with a newfound boldness in Christ. Thank you for your sacrifice on the cross and may the significance of that one act by you, Jesus, forever be etched upon our minds and hearts. Amen.*

I Hope I Don't Forget This

Genesis 50:15-21

"*Realizing that their father was dead, Joseph's brother said, 'What if Joseph still bears a grudge against us and pays us back in full for all the wrong we did to him?' So they approached Joseph saying, 'Your father gave this instruction before he died. Say to Joseph, I beg you, forgive the crime of your brothers and the wrong they did in harming you. Now, therefore, please forgive the crime of the servants of the God of your father.' Joseph wept when they spoke to him. Then his brothers also wept, fell down before him and said, 'we are here as your slaves.' But Joseph said to them, 'Don't be afraid. Am I in the place of God, even though you intended to do harm to me, God intended it for good in order to preserve a numerous people as he is doing today. So have no fear. I myself will provide for you and your little ones.' In this way he reassured them speaking kindly to me.*"

Romans 8:37-39

"*Knowing all these things we are more than conquerors through Him who loved us for I am convinced that neither death, nor life, nor angels, nor rulers, nor things present, nor things to come, nor powers, nor height, nor depth, nor anything else in all creation will be able to separate us from the love of God in Christ Jesus our Lord."*

When you travel all the time, it is good to get help from people. Fred Gabory is a successful business man and he wanted to use his frequent flyer miles for us to go California. He said we could also stay on the Concierge floor of the Hilton Hotel in Anaheim, California."

I spend about a third of my life in a tent on a sandbar by a river in the jungle. The idea of staying on the Concierge floor of the Hilton Hotel in Anaheim, California is as high as the cotton's going to get in my life. So I said, "Fred, I'd love to do that."

Fred and I flew there. There's a three-hour time difference from Atlanta to Los Angeles. That means when it is 9:00 p.m. in Los Angeles, it feels like midnight to me. I got back to my hotel about 10:30 p.m. which is pretty late for someone my age (about 1:30 in the morning to me physically).

I have worked in jungles for about 25 years. Jungles are hot and buggy, and I have learned that if I don't wear much to sleep in, I am more comfortable out in the jungle. Do you understand what I am trying to say? This is a habit that is carried over to the way I sleep in the United States.

I have also learned that when you reach my age that people my age usually don't sleep all night long; we have to get up and find an outhouse in the middle of the night.

So I got up to go find the bathroom, and I walked right out my hotel door, locked myself in the hallway in the all-and-all. There is not anyone to help me! I am pounded on the door.... nothing worked.

I remembered that at the end of the hall and around the corner there is a lady sitting at a desk and she just loves to say "May I help you?" I thought that lady could help me about now. I started down the middle of the hall, none of this slinking along the side for me, no sir! Right down the middle of the hall. I got to where I was just about to make the turn and the elevator door, right in front of me, goes "ding" and I stood my ground! I am not sure how I did it, but I just stood there. I knew I was about to come face-to-face with the entire Yazoo City Mississippi Chapter of the Women's Christian Temperance Union.

Slowly the elevator door opened and out stepped a security guard. He looked at me and said, "Well, I've seen it all now." I said, "Yes, you have. Now let it back in his room."

"What room are you in?" I didn't have a clue, but I couldn't tell him so I said, "I'm in room 1414." He said, "No problem mister. Let's go." We walked down the hall together, and I was so grateful there were no video cameras filming this episode, and, in my mind, I'm praying, "Oh Lord, please let this be my room."

We got to room 1414 and he knocked. Nothing happened. He knocked a little harder. Nothing happened. He put the pass key in the door, opened the door, and we peak inside, and "praise the Lord" it was my room!

I sat on the edge of the bed laughing at myself. I sat there thinking you can't find the bathroom, you don't remember what room you're in, and you are getting old!!!

Then it dawned on me, I'm not getting old at all. I'm getting busy, and I am so busy someone explained to me after early worship that what I have is called "data overload." There is too much stuff going in here, and I can't keep it in. Does this happen to you? I find that I get so busy that not everything fits in here, and the stuff that falls out is some pretty important stuff.

We just had our ROW dinner down in Atlanta. Andre Crouch came and sang for the dinner and it was really Amazing. Rod Stewart showed up at the end of our dinner, amazingly enough, he just happened to be in town. You really never know who is coming to these things. One of our Trustees, Rick Justice, was there. His wife is named Rose, and they live in Meridian, Mississippi on a farm.

They have a Pekinese named Snuffy and a pot-bellied pig named Hogburt who lives in the house with them. They have a lady named Miss Annie who helps look after the house, a man named Cleve looks after the farm. At the barn they have a 200-pound Bull Mastiff named Babe.

On a cold January morning, Rose is dressed up and ready for the day. She is getting ready to go into town and she decides before she leaves for town she is going to let the little pig out in the backyard to do his thing, and then she will head off to town. Rose lets the little pig out without knowing that up at the barn, Cleve has let the great big dog out of the barn. The great big dog sees the little, bitty pig and he thinks one word, "lunch." The great big dog runs down and he grabs that little bitty pig and starts shaking him in his mouth. The pig starts screaming. Rose comes running out of the house yelling at that dog to drop the pig. The dog drops the pig, the pig jumps in the lake and starts to swim away. Cleve comes running down from the barn and Rose is yelling, "Cleve, swim out there and save my pig." Cleve starts unbuttoning my shirt on this freezing cold January morning when Snuffy the Pekinese sees an opportunity of a lifetime.

Snuffy can't stand that great big Bull Mastiff. The little Pekinese comes running out of the house, runs up behind the great big dog, jumps up in the air and goes CHOMP and grabs that great big dog. The big dog is screaming, running around in circles trying to shake off the Pekinese, the pig is swimming off in the distance, Miss Annie is calling upon the name of the Lord, Cleve is unbuttoning his shirt, and Rose is saying, "Cleve, swim out there and save my pig!" Cleve says, "Rose, I would be glad to, but I can't swim."

The wife of a Presbyterian elder, all dressed up and ready for the day in Meridian, Mississippi on a cold January morning makes the decision of a lifetime. Rose just jumps in that lake and starts swimming to save her little pig. She said it was just like a football game, "You know throwing the pig skin." That's her line, not mine.

She said she grabbed that pig and threw him and he thought it was a game. He swam back to her, and she grabbed him, threw him, and he'd swim back to her. She said she was finally able to pitch that little pig out of the lake and she said she collapsed on the side of the lake like a "beached whale." She looked at me and said, "Mathes, there are some things worth dying for."

As much as I laughed at her story, I couldn't help but agree with her. There are some things in life worth dying for, but there are a whole lot of things in life worth living for, and I know that I get all this data overload, and life gets so busy I get so busy that I forget that there are things worth dying for, and I forget that there are things worth living for and today what I want us to talk about is the very thing that gets in the way of most of us living a full Christian life. It is exactly what Paul left out of our text this morning.

Paul says:

> "Knowing all these things we are more than conquerors through Him who loved us for I am convinced that neither death, nor life, nor angels, nor rulers, nor things present, nor things to come, nor powers, nor height, nor depth, nor anything else in all creation will be able to separate us from the love of God in Christ Jesus our Lord."

Paul left out the thing that holds most of us back. Paul left out the past. He includes the present and the future, but not the past. Paul struggled with his past in the way that he "was", just like so many of us struggle with our past.

Mark Twain said, "The inability to forget is much worse than the inability to remember." Now you think about that just for a second. You hear a sermon. You see some wonderful presentation. The kids sing great music and dance. You cannot help but be lifted up by all of that and you think, maybe God can use me. Maybe there is something I can do for the Lord around our church or somewhere in the world. Maybe there is something I can give, do, or say.

There is some way that I can serve, and we walk over and we start to pick up the phone and say put me to work and we get about "this" close to the phone and we remember that we got caught and we think everyone heard about it, or we remember that we got away with it. It still clips at your heels, but you got away with it, but it still chews on you. Or, we remember that somebody called us a name, or they left us, or they broke our hearts, or they were mean to us, we remember something out of our past and we just walk away from the phone, don't we?

How did Joseph's brothers feel when they heard he was in charge? First of all, what happened to Joseph? His brothers sold him into slavery and now he turns out to be in charge. How did his brothers feel? Were they just thrilled to go see their brother? They were scared to death, weren't they? They were scared of their past. That is what it does to a lot of us. It holds you back because we are afraid someone is going to find out.

Your past can be as recent as last night. Your past can be yesterday. Those are all in the past. Our past scares some of us, doesn't it? So, we don't step up to the plate because we are afraid someone is going to find out.

Let's talk about how to handle fear. One of the places we serve is called the Congo. It is as big as everything east of the Mississippi River. It is huge. It is also caught in the middle of a horrible civil war.

My ship was stolen by the army of the Congo, and my men were taken hostage. The army of Uganda agreed to take me in, set my men free, and sink my ship. Thankfully, I did not have to go, and my men escaped. The army kept my ship. We wanted to steal it back, but we could not, so we sank our ship right out from under the army of the Congo and made them MAD!! The rebel movement now controls our area.

The man who is the President of that rebel movement that controls 30 million people sat in a plane next to me, rode in my canoe with me, slept in my tent with me, and we shared machine guns together, and we came the 100 miles down the San Karu River in the middle of this war. We preached the gospel, immunized children, treated sickness in the remote jungle villages, and at the end of the 100 miles there is a village called Bena Dibele.

Bena Dibele is on top of a mountain. On the top of that mountain there was a truck waiting for us to carry us out of this war. We strapped our gear on our backs, and we took foot lockers in each hand, and we teamed up to carry all of our gear to the top of this mountain only to discover that our truck had broken down in the jungle on the other side of the river and we were trapped in the Congo. We cannot go up stream because the motor is not powerful enough. There is nowhere to land a plane. There is no plane to come and get us. We are stuck in the middle of this war.

I have a picture where we all have our arms around some of the soldiers. We took this picture and then I slaughtered a goat. We ate this goat together, sat around talking about the war and about *Rivers of the World*. I had some little ROW bracelets I gave the soldiers. They were dark green, and they matched the camouflage and the soldiers thought it looked good. They modeled their bracelets and the garrison commander sat down and said, "I have made a decision. I have a truck, and you can use my truck to escape this war."

At 2:00 p.m. in the afternoon, we have about four hours of daylight to go 100 miles through the jungle. We make the decision to go as fast as we can drive and make all the noise we can make with the hopes that enemy soldiers will think we are a supply truck.

We piled all of our gear into the back of one pick-up truck. We all sat on an edge that is no wider than the edge of a pew. After 100 miles traveling through the jungle, we were bounced to death. It was horribly painful!

There were machine guns all around. The rebel soldiers, Congo soldiers, and my guys, one of whom was a chaplain, were on our way out. I asked chaplain to pray for us as we left.

Everyone was scared. I reached for my camera and passed it around for everyone to say goodbye to the families. If we are killed, at least they will find the tape and know we were thinking about them. I thought that would cheer everybody up!

The first time the camera went around everyone thought it was hilarious, but the second time it was not funny anymore. We kept on going and another hour later, I looked at my folks and they were still scared.

When I get scared I sing. I have done this for 25 years. I sing, "I wish I was in the land of cotton, old times...." It is a song called *Dixie*!

Try to imagine me zooming through the jungle singing *Dixie* at the top of my lungs! It helped for a while. Then we got out and had to stretch our legs and they told us we were going to cross six bridges, but all the bridges had been blown up and then rebuilt out of bamboo.

Where I come from we fish with bamboo. We don't build bridges out of it, but the driver decided if he backs up and goes as fast as he can go we will not weigh as much and we will get across the bridge. We took the tracks off a blown up tank and we lay them across this bridge, he backed up, hit it as fast as we could go, and we get across all six bridges and make it to the other side.

Then the road disappeared altogether. The truck is going up two sides and down, two sides and down, and we are getting banged all up. We hit a particularly bad bump and everything goes WHAM, and someone screamed, and I thought he had broken something.

We hit another one and he screamed again, but this time he screamed, "Is that all you've got? Then give me some more!" We looked at him as we hit another bad bump and he screamed, "Is that all you've got? Then give me some more!" Before you know it this whole truck is zooming through the jungle and at every bad bump we are screaming out, "Is that all you've got?" Clap, Clap. "Then give me some more!" Clap. Clap. Over and over again.

We got to a place called Lojo from Bena Dibele. We got there, and we had no food for two days. We sucked water out of little mud puddles to have something to drink. We lived to learn about fear.

For some of us, the past is last night. For some of us, the past started September 11th. For some of us, we are scared when we see a plane fly by. We are scared when we see folks from specific countries. We are scared when we have to go to the airport and travel. We are scared to spend money or give. We are scared.

Let me tell you what I learned about fear. We faced a lot of fear on that trip, and we started by praying. We prayed at that fear really hard, then when we took off, that fear did not go away. We made a video and thought about our families.

We did not come back and say, "Oh Ben, I'm all alone in life." That does not apply to me that is silly. You may be by yourself, but you are not alone. You hear me? You may be by yourself, but you are not alone. You are surrounded by people right here who will face any fear you have with you. You just have to let them know what you need.

Then we sang. I have sung *Dixie* for 25 years and I will sing it until I'm gone. When I am by myself I sing, *Jesus Loves Me*. In front of my men, I sing *Dixie*.

When fear did not go away what did we do? We started chanting. "Is that all you've got? Then give me some more." Why? Because of what Paul said, I also said, I am convinced that there is not anything in all creation that can separate us from the love of God in Christ Jesus. There is a lot of courage in that. I hope I do not forget that and I hope you don't as well. God bless you and thank you for the courage you give me.

I've had Enough

Ephesians 3:14-21 and 4:1 (NRSV)

"For this reason, I bow my knees before the Father, from whom every family in heaven and on earth takes its name. I pray that, according to the riches of his glory, He may grant that you may be strengthened in your inner being with power through His Spirit, and that Christ may dwell in your hearts through faith, as you are being rooted and grounded in love. I pray that you may have the power to comprehend, with all the saints, what is the breadth and length and height and depth, and to know the love of Christ that surpasses knowledge, so that you may be filled with all the fullness of God. Now to him who by the power at work within us is able to accomplish abundantly far more than all we can ask or imagine, to Him he glory in the church and in Christ Jesus to all generations, forever and ever. Amen. I, therefore, the prisoner in the Lord, beg you to lead a life worthy of the calling to which you have been called."

We finished our radio station in Belize. It is reaching 50,000 people a day, but I did not come to tell you about that. We finished our base camp in Belize, started new work in Vietnam, Brazil, and Kenya, but I did not come to tell you about all of that either. We even started new work in Ecuador, but, again, I did not come to tell you about that. I

Am I Ever Going to Get Out of Here?

did come to tell you about what happened to us in the Democratic Republic of the Congo (DRC).

A fellow named Andrae Crouch wrote two of the songs in your green hymn book. Andrae wrote a song for Rivers of the World (ROW), followed by Ray Charles, Aretha Franklin, Billy Joel, Kim Waters, Otis Redding and Pete Seger, all of whom gave us river songs. It enabled me to put $60,000 in cash in my backpack and to bury a half a pound of gold in my belt. With these provisions, we flew from Atlanta to Rwanda, Africa.

Upon arrival, I took my big African knife, tucked it under my armpit, and went behind a warehouse with two Russian soldiers with machine guns to negotiate. The Russians thought I was crazy, and I thought they were a little off, but they had a great big troop transport plane. I chartered that plane and we filled it with a hospital, literally a ton of French Bibles, 10 drums of gasoline, and my crew. The Russians flew us right into the middle of the war in the Congo We landed on a dirt strip and worked at a hospital, which today is serving 200,000 people in the center of the Democratic Republic of the Congo (DRC). Somebody say Amen! But, that is not what I came to tell you about!

I came to tell you about what happened once we finished working in the hospital. We loaded all of our crew into a great big 40-foot-long dug-out canoe, and we went up the Sankuru River for a couple of days. We set up our camp on a sandbar. We put our tents beside the river and we bathed in the river along with hippos and crocodiles. We began each day by heading off into remote villages to do ministry. One village we visited was Kongolulu. It looked like something out of a Tarzan movie because it is located on top of an escarpment. We carried a generator, medicine, and footlockers of Bibles to the top of the escarpment. We went into this village and first held a worship service, then we did a medical clinic because everybody was sick with either parasites, malaria, worms or river blindness, or a combination of these ailments. We tried to treat everyone in the village.

Late in the day we hung a sheet in the trees and we showed a movie. We put the generator behind a hut, ran a long extension cord out so they didn't hear the generator, and we showed a movie called *The Jesus Film*, depicting the life of Christ. Keep in mind that these are people who know that movies exist, but they had never seen one. Can you image how spellbound you would be if a movie unfolded before you for the first time?

So here we are watching the movie, and I am taking photographs of the folks who were watching the movie and then it happened! It was late in the day, and off in the distance I see this massive African thunderstorm moving right between these two large mountains.

Now, our storms in the States start with gray clouds followed by rain. These African thunderstorms roll right up on you just like a bowling ball. As I was watched this storm, I just knew that if it came barreling into this village, all of those people were going to run and hide because they are scared of storms. This meant they would not be able to see *The Jesus Film*. That thought really bothered me, so I stood there and said, "Storm, I have come all the way from Georgia to show these people this movie. If you come blowing in here you are going to ruin the whole thing, so you just stay right there."

One of my men named Mike Reinsel walked up to me and said, "Ben, what are you doing?" I said, "Well, in the Book they call this rebuking the storm. You stand here and rebuke this storm with me." He said, "Okay." And we stood there and talked to this storm.

Now you can do what you want with this, but two and a half hours later that storm was still sitting there over those mountains. We were able to show *The Jesus Film*! But when we began packing everything up and heading down the escarpment, the storm began moving right toward us. Trees were bending over, lightning was streaking all the way across the sky and the thunder was shaking our bones. We had to get in a dugout canoe and travel up river a couple of miles in the middle of this storm. We were all huddled in our canoe singing hymns and praying! I was in the back of the boat praying, "Lord, I just bought all this camera equipment. Now, if you hit us with lightning you are going to expect me to save Chris Price, a pastor in Atlanta. I want you to know something, Lord, I cannot hold onto the camera equipment and Chris. So, here's the deal. If you hit us with lightning, Chris is going to drown because I cannot let go of this camera equipment."

We made it to our camp and it looked like a scene out of the *Wizard of Oz*. Our tents were rolling down the sand bar. Pappa Akula, one of our Congo staff, tried to cover our food and save whatever he could. We dove out of the canoe, ran 300 to 400 yards to try and capture our tents and bring them back. People were living in tents to get out of the storm. Chris Price and his 19-year-old daughter came running up to me saying their tent had disappeared. They were wondering what they should do. I told them to dive into my tent with me. They dove in and Chris' 19-year-old daughter sat up and said, "Ewww Ben, this tent is nasty. It stinks in here and it is full of sand. I cannot stay in here." She made me pull all of my stuff out of the tent so I could pick and shake all the sand out so this child could get inside my tent. When I finished that, her father showed up with a footlocker, which had sleeping pads. I didn't even have a sleeping pad! He pulled out two sleeping pads, two sleeping bags, and in the middle of a war in the heart of Africa this Presbyterian minister pulled out two great big, satin pillows! Chris and his daughter climbed into my tent and the two of them fell sound to sleep, snoring like lumberjacks!

I tried to climb into my two-man tent and there was just so much room for a man my size! I discovered Chris and his daughter had pushed all my stuff over to the side and I could not even straighten my legs out. I was lying there going, "You know, Lord, what did I do to deserve this?" The Lord said, "You remember that storm?" I said, "Yep, can't miss it. Can't miss it." The Lord said, "You know when that storm was brewing, you could have told it to go away, but you didn't, so I let that storm just stay there and then I let that storm follow you out of the village. I let it chase you down to the river, and I let that storm destroy your camp. Now I'm going to let Chris and Lauren and this storm keep you awake all night long so you can think about the fact that you have grown comfortable in your faith and your faith was not strong enough to tell the storm to go away."

Well, the next morning, I told that to Chris and we laughed. We pretty much agreed that our relationship with the Lord is a lot like our relationship with people we love. You pretty much know what to expect out of your family. And you know what not to expect. You know when you are going to be affectionate and when you are not. You know when you are going to say your prayers and when you probably will not say your prayers. We fall into a routine about those things that we like and we fall into routines about things we don't like.

Do you have traffic here like we do in Atlanta? How many of you will have to contend with traffic tomorrow? Do you just love it? No, I'm sure you don't, but we get used to it, don't we? Now, you are not going to believe this, but I have people who work around the world with me and a great number of them complain about things. It is too hot, there are too many bugs, I don't feel good, and, oh my, is that a crocodile? I mean the list goes on and on.

Now don't raise your hand, instead just blink at me. Do you have someone in your life who loves to complain? I have a new thing that I have started when I get around people who complain. You can complain around me all you want to, but you have to end the complaint by saying, "And that's just the way I like it." Think about it. Oh, it's so hot out here and that's just the way I like it. I don't feel very good and that's just the way I like it. Is that a hippo, oh well, that's just the way I like it. Try this with me. I'll say something and you answer back, "That's just the way I like it." Let's try this.

Gee, my relationship with the Lord sure is dull. "That's just the way I like it."

I can't stand what I do for a living. "That's just the way I like it."

My kids are driving me crazy. "That's just the way I like it."

The sermon is almost over. "That's just the way I like it."

You see, I think this is what happened with the church at Ephesus. Paul loved that church, but I think they just had gotten used to each other and sort of fell into a routine and that is why he wrote to them. That is why Paul said, "Look, Christian I pray for you every day that you will know the height, the breadth, the length, and the depth of the love of Christ that just surpasses knowledge. I pray for you every day that you will be filled with the very fullness of God."

I travel to about 200 cities a year, a dozen countries around the world, and I meet some wonderful people. I did a conference in what I call Middle America, kind of where Missouri and Kansas come together. The young people in this conference had gone off to Kansas to paint a church. The folks at this conference gave me someone to drive me out to Kansas and back, three hours one way and three hours back. I climbed in the van with my new friend and I soon discovered he had this habit. He ended every single sentence by saying, "so..." For instance, "Yeah, I got a wife and a couple of kids, so…Church is really important to me, so… Yeah, I work in a factory, so…" I sat there thinking, "Lord, if I have to listen to this for six hours, I'm going to scream!" The Lord said, "So…"

It was just a habit. This fellow had no idea he was doing this. Paul had a habit. When Paul couldn't think of anything else to say, he would say "now." In the Book he said, "Now, give glory to God in Christ Jesus and the Church forever and ever. Amen." That's good. He added some other stuff to it. "Now to the God who by the power at work within you…to that God be glory in Christ Jesus and the Church forever and ever. Amen." That's better. If Paul had been a Southerner he would have said, "Right now give glory to God who right now by the power at work within you right now can do more with you right now than you ever dreamed or imagined, to that God be glory in Christ Jesus and the Church forever and ever. Amen."

When Paul said those things it became a whole other issue. You mean, right now? The Book says I can be doing more than I ever dreamed or imagined. You're probably thinking, "Ben, if the Word is true, then how come my life is just so…? How come I hurt so deeply inside? How come I don't feel like anyone loves me? Or that I even matter? How come I keep repeating the same sin over and over again?" I would say to you; Christian did you know that the Lord could walk right up to you with a tray containing a fulfilling life. This life would include the knowledge, the height, the breadth, the length, the fulfilling love of God in Jesus Christ, a life of service and ministry and compassion and a life overflowing with the fruits of the Spirit. The Lord could walk right up and hand that to you and you could basically sit on it and squelch the Holy Spirit. You could even say to God, "You know Lord, I know a very fulfilling and challenging life is available, but I have grown so accustomed to feeling guilty. It is normal for me to not feel loved or important. I have grown used to doing the same things over and over again and beating myself up about them. I think I will just keep that life because that is really just the way I like it."

What Paul was talking about actually puts some of the responsibility back on us, doesn't it? The hospital that we worked on in the DRC had been created from an old hospital that had been standing there. The army of the Congo prepared the hospital for us and as they retreated they ripped off all the doors and they burned them for firewood. They burned all of our French nursing textbooks. I have 35 nursing students who have handwritten textbooks because our professor's hand wrote the text books before they forgot them. The army of the Congo burned them all. They took machine guns and they shot up all the buildings and they shot out all the windows, so on opening day of our hospital, we put the word out that we would have a free clinic for everybody!

Six hundred mothers signed the paper that they were coming. We do not know how many showed up only that 600 signed the paper. Each mother brought an armload of babies. We found a room that still had a door on it. They did not shove the door open, instead, these women ripped the doors off the hinges to get to us. As graphic as that was, the picture that stayed on my heart was of a tall, very thin,

African mother who had a tiny little baby and she was standing beside a shattered, shot out hospital window. She took this tiny little baby, she fed the baby through the broken glass and she held out her long arm, begging us to take the baby and give it a chance to live.

When Paul said, "I beg you to live the life you were called to live" is the same word as that mother who begged us to take her child. Paul's words speak to you and to me that it is all about hope. Life, and your circumstances, do not have to stay this way. If you are aching inside or if you feel needless, empty or worthless, it does not have to stay that way and it begins when you finally get alone with the Lord and you say, "You know Lord, I've had enough. I've had enough of repeating sin, feeling empty, feeling down in the dumps. I've had enough of feeling like I'm just waiting to die. If your Word is true, then push me out of the way and give me a sense of the very fullness of your love. Give me the courage to step up to the plate."

I'll tell you what I did. ROW has a new ship in Brazil. I am so excited about it. I went with the Presbyterian Church of Brazil and we traveled the Amazon River. What language do they speak in Brazil? Portuguese. I speak a language called "Southernese." Those are two different "languages." I made up my mind that when the Brazilians wanted to have Bible study and when they wanted to pray, I would take this one verse of Scripture and I would read it over and over and over for two weeks. I kept reading, "And now to Him who by the power at work within you." Let me tell you, when I wake up at 3:30 in the morning and I want to toss and turn about the same things you want to toss and turnabout, when

I want to look at my world and feel defeated and overwhelmed, when I want to start doubting and say how in the world can we do these things, you know what happens? That verse comes right back up in my heart and I hear Paul saying to me, "Ben, right now, give glory to the God who right now can do more with you than you ever dreamed or imagined." And you know what? Then I can fall right back to sleep and that is just the way I like it.

Lord, Jesus, teach me every day to look for ways in which you demonstrate your vast love to me. Help me to not be satisfied with my life or my current circumstances, but instead to accept fully the abundant life you desire for me. Help me to be content, but never settling for less than what you want for my life. Precious Lord, may I dream dreams that only you can fulfill. Place within my heart your plans and purposes for my life and allow me to clearly walk in the way you have designed for me from even before the beginning of my life. Thank you, God that your promises are sure and they are true. In Jesus' name I pray, Amen.

Not Just Yet

Luke 9

I love Luke 9. Allow me to walk you through some of it before we get to our passage for the day. It begins with Jesus calling the 12 disciples together. He gives them power and authority over all demons, to cure diseases, and then He sends them out to proclaim the Kingdom of God and to heal. He tells them not to take anything with them. Whatever house will let you stay, stay there, Jesus instructed. If you are not welcome, knock the dust off your feet and keep on walking.

The disciples made quite an impact. We do not know what they did, but we do know that they made such an impact that Herod the governor actually heard about all that was taking place. Now, what would it take for you to go out of your house on foot and do something so good that the governor of your state would hear about it? Keep this comparison in mind. What the disciples were doing was so good that Herod heard about it. I love what the Word says, "He was perplexed." He did not know if it was John the Baptist who had come back from the dead, if it was Elijah or one of the other prophets. Herod was just really confused and wanted to find out what was going on.

The 12 disciples returned from their travels and they gathered to tell Jesus all that they had done. Wouldn't you just love to have been a fly on the wall for that? Imagine the stories: the blind see, the lame walk, the deaf hear, diseases are cured, and demons are cast out. Think about that. What an exciting and obviously overwhelming time to be with Jesus. The crowds found out about Him and they just swarmed Him. They were everywhere! People were all around Jesus just waiting to hear what He had to say and waiting to be cured. It is just amazing! At the end of the day, they were all hungry and the disciples said, "Oh send them off somewhere." And Jesus said, "No you feed them." And He fed 5,000 people.

Through the power and authority of Jesus, the disciples were able to heal the sick, cast out demons, and feed the hungry. You cannot tell me that Matthew and Judas were not sitting there thinking, "Man, this is something really great. We can make a lot of money off of this! This is awfully exciting!" And then Jesus brought it all down to earth. He always does that. Jesus brought it into focus when He asked the big question, "Who do others say that I am?" The disciples said, "Well, we hear the crowds saying you are John the Baptist, you're Elijah, or you are one of the prophets." Then Jesus looked at the 12 men who were closest to Him and He said, "Well, who do you say that I am?"

We do not know if there was silence do we? Scripture cannot say "silence." We don't know if some walked away, if they bent over and adjusted their sandals. We do not know how long it took, but we do know that finally it was Peter who stepped up to the plate and Peter is the one who said, "You are the Christ; the Son of the Living God." That is when Jesus reveals what it takes to be an effective disciple. Listen to what He said:

> *"And He was saying to them all, 'If anyone wishes to come after me, he must deny himself, and take up his cross daily and follow me. For whoever wishes to save his life will lose it, but whoever loses his life for my sake, he is the one who will save it. For what is a man profited if he gains the whole world, and loses or forfeits himself? For whoever is ashamed of me and my words, the Son of Man will be ashamed of him when He comes in His glory, and the glory of the Father and of the holy angels. But I say to you truthfully, there are some of those standing here who will not taste death until they see the Kingdom of God." Luke 9:23-27 (NASB)*

Wow! What a powerful passage of Scripture. If any of you want to be my disciples, let them deny themselves, take up their cross daily, and follow me. Oh, the first thing you always have to hear is the Good News. He does not say, "Take up your cross and forever follow me." Forever would make these big pronouncements about your life just too overwhelming. Jesus just says one day at a time. Just for today, I want you to follow me. Just for today, deny yourself, take up your cross, and follow me. Do not make these outlandish promises about how you are going to change and how you are going to grow because that takes more than one day. But, for today, if you want to be close to Jesus, deny yourself, take up your cross, and follow Him. That is a military term that means He will be in charge of your life. All you have to do is follow where He wants you to go. I love that!

Let's examine further the idea of taking up your cross. You know and I know that forever and a day preachers have blamed your sin on that cross. The cross represents your sins, the things you have done wrong in your life, and it is just awful that you must carry this with you from now on. I'm sorry but that is the most ridiculous thing I have ever heard!

The cross that Christ begs us to carry is not the guilt and weight of our sin. That is not how the Lord operates. If that bursts your religious bubble, then let's just start over. The cross the Lord wants you to carry is very simple. It implies not being selfish. For today, daily, one day at a time, decide not to be selfish with your spiritual gifts. If you have been given the gift of compassion or healing or listening or encouraging, then heal, listen, encourage, and show compassion. If you have been given financial gifts, obviously, then write a check. Give away some of your money and do something good in this world. If you have been given a talent, use that talent to build up someone in the name of Jesus Christ, but above everything else, if you want to be closer to the Lord today, then deny yourself the joy of ignorance about the needs of those around you.

Oh, I have to say that again. If you want to be an effective disciple of Jesus Christ, then just for today, deny yourself the joy of ignorance about the needs of those around you. If I did not know that my brother was hurting, I would not reach out to him. If I did not know that the child right over there was hungry, I would not feed that child. If I did not know about those orphans in Vietnam, I would not try to raise money to look after those children and I could walk around in ignorant bliss. But, for today, I am going to take the burden of hope that is mine, place it upon my heart and proclaim that I am part of the answer and that because of Jesus, I am not part of the problem and today I am going to do something about it. How about you?

You're probably thinking, "Okay, Ben, I hear you. I am going to do all that stuff that makes sense to me. I am going to do this daily one-day-at-a-time thing. I am going to show more compassion. I am going to give more money. I am going to get more involved. I am going to be closer to my wife. I am going to spend more time with my kids. I am going to do all those things, Ben. I am going to do it, but well…not just yet." Why? "Because I have got to get that promotion at the office. I have to recoup my IRA. We have got to get out of all these wars. I have to see the economy get a little more stable and then I promise you, when those things happen, I will step closer to the Lord, but just not yet!"

Peggy Rambo was a dear, precious friend of mine, a missionary who served 30 some odd years in the Democratic Republic of the Congo (DRC). We had one of those old Ford Broncos. You know the ones we really liked, the square ones. It was driven by Johnny Miller from South Africa all the way up to the DRC. It was just an incredible truck! I do not know how many times I have driven that thing. Well, this was just one more day for Baba Peggy. Peggy took that truck and she backed it up to the little shed that was hers. She opened the tailgate. Remember it had a tailgate…that was so cool. She did what she always did. She bent down and groaning she would pick up three or four foot lockers and slide them into the back of that Ford Bronco.

One foot locker had seeds for vegetables and corn. It also had some hand trowels. Another foot locker had tape measures and scales for weighing and measuring babies. It also had some baby formula, but not much. It mainly had some antibiotics and worm medicine, things like that. Additionally, it contained report cards to give to parents so that they would know how their children were doing. Another foot locker had gospel tracts in it and the last foot locker had food and some water for her and perhaps a blanket in case the truck broke down and she got stuck out in the jungle.

Peggy said she loaded the truck up just like always and she headed off into the bush. She went to what was a clearing in the elephant grass, and Peggy said she drove up and there were 16 African mothers and their babies sitting on these long benches just waiting for her to appear. She stepped out of the truck and she greeted them by saying "Mbote" and they all said "Mbote," meaning "hello" in their native language of Lingala. Everybody just smiled and laughed. They exchanged some pleasantries. She walked along and she picked up each baby and looked at each one and talked about the beauty of each child. There were always one or two who had some special needs. She took the foot lockers and she began at one end and she walked her way through a presentation. She had some seeds and some trowels. She did not give it away, but if a woman had a penny, oddly enough the hand trowel would cost a penny. This would give the woman a tool that would enable her to feed her family.

Peggy said she did fine throughout that entire experience. She packed everything up, she put it back in the truck, she closed the tailgate, she turned and she looked at those 16 wonderful African mothers and this is what she said, "We don't have enough money to buy the gasoline to keep all of these clinics open and we have had to make some difficult decisions. I'm afraid that this is the last time that I will be with you. I'm sorry. We simply don't have the money to buy the gasoline." Peggy said she looked into the faces of 16 horrified African mothers and she did all right. She turned around and got in the Bronco and she said she did all right. She started the Bronco and still, she did all right. She pulled slowly down that dirt road and she said she did just fine until she looked in the rear view mirror and running through the dust that was kicked up by her Bronco as she drove down that dirt road came an African mother clutching her baby like a football, running behind the truck and screaming at the top of her lungs, "If you leave my baby will die!"

We hear about those needs and we say, "Well, Ben, not just yet." What does the Lord say? The Lord comes back and says, "If you are ashamed of me now, I will be ashamed of you when I come into my kingdom." He is not teasing. This is not a game. The Lord wants to know on whose team you reside. Who do you stand up for? What is your priority in the world? Is it one more deposit to your IRA or standing closer to the Lord and denying yourself the ignorance of the needs of those around you? As difficult as that is, we have the wonderful news from Jesus that says, "But, there are some of you reading this who will not taste death before you see the Kingdom of God."

Dr. David Seel, who was a Presbyterian medical missionary to South Korea, wrote a book about his years as a cancer surgeon at Jesus Hospital, also known as the Presbyterian Medical Center in Chonju, South Korea. In this book, Dr. Seel said, "Can I possibly remember that every face in the long parade of patients deserves the same kindness, respect, and compassion that I would show to Jesus himself? Can I possibly remember that every face in the long parade is my Lord?"

When we can look at the people around us with the same love, hope, compassion, and joy that we would look at Jesus, then our eyes have seen the Kingdom of God. Your choice is simple. Who do you say that Jesus is? Elijah, Jeremiah, one of the prophets? If you stand with Peter and say "You are the Christ, the Son of the living God" then this day, the challenge for you is to deny yourself, take up your cross, and follow Him, for in so doing, you will see the Kingdom of God. Amen.

> *Jesus, I pray that you become more to me than just my Savior. Be Lord of my life. I ask that you break my heart for those things that break yours. Do not merely give me eyes to see those in need around me, but also give to me a willing spirit, a compassionate heart and an immediate obedience to meet those needs. Father, teach me how to really take up my cross and follow after your Son, Jesus. Help me to know the depths of sacrifice necessary to become like Christ and in so doing, I too will know the joy of being raised with Him in glory. Amen.*

One Day Closer

Psalm 118:21-25

"I thank you that you have answered me and I become my salvation. The stone that the builders rejected has become the chief cornerstone. This is the Lord's doing. It is marvelous in our eyes. This is the day the Lord has made, let us rejoice and be glad in it. Save us, we beseech you, oh Lord. Oh Lord we beseech you, give us success."

I am not allowed to fix anything in my house. I am pretty good with a gun and a knife, but a hammer and a screwdriver spells disaster for me. I was standing in the kitchen and I saw water dripping out of my refrigerator/freezer on the freezer side. That cannot be good. I opened the thing and it looked like a group of Eskimos had moved in there. There was frost over everything and I did not have a clue what was happening, so I pulled the ice bucket out of the freezer. I dumped the ice in the sink. I set the ice bucket on top of the washing machine and I decided to deal with this later on. I go on about my business and I come back later and I am on the phone talking with someone on my staff and I hear the ice maker make the noise it makes when it dumps ice out of the ice tray into the ice bucket thingy. I look in the sink and there is no ice bucket. I look over on the washing machine and low and behold there is the ice bucket. Well, that means that my ice maker has just dumped ice, willy-nilly, into the freezer compartment of my refrigerator freezer. I have been gone for a week. That means that for an entire week my ice maker has faithfully been dumping ice into my freezer and there is nothing to catch it.

I get off the phone and decided I was not going to get mad at myself. This is too much fun and I realized there are two ways to deal with this issue. I can either go over and get a trash can, put it by the freezer, open the door slowly and try to catch some of the avalanche or I could just grab the freezer door, yank it open, and let's just see what happens. Well, you know what I did. I went and got a broom and dust pan and I decided just to yank the freezer door open. It looked like I had robbed the ice department at a 7-11. Ice came pouring out all over the floor. There were millions of pieces of ice everywhere. I started laughing and I started sweeping the stuff into the dust pan. I will have picked up this one and this one and this one and dumped it in the sink. I will pick up this one, this one, and I will dump them in the sink. I will pick up this one, this one, and this one, dump them in the sink. I will get this one and this one and you know what, this is what my life looks like. It is in a million pieces and instead of being scattered all over the floor, it is scattered all over the world! I am going to pick up this one, this one, this one, and this is the day that the Lord has made! Let's us rejoice and be glad in it. Yeah, right.

Do you know why preachers say that verse all the time? We say it because we can remember it. Come on, I want you to try it. Say it with me. "This is the day the Lord has made, let us rejoice and be glad in it." Now if you are like most folks, you said that without even cracking a smile. I can see you, even though this is the printed page. To rejoice means to stand up and spin around in joy. I did not see any spinning around and joy out there, but I did decide I had better go back and look at the 118th Psalm and see what the Lord wants me to learn and share from those good words. So I did.

Now the problem with Psalms is that they usually go on forever. They have words in them we do not understand or they repeat themselves and it is really hard to find the flow. So, if you do not mind, I would like to give you a short version of the 118th Psalm. Here is how it goes:

> *"Oh give thanks to the Lord for He is good. His steadfast love endures forever. Out of my distress I call on the Lord and the Lord answered me. With the Lord on my side, I don't fear anybody. The Lord is on my side to help me. All the nations surrounded me and in the name of the Lord, I cut them off. They surrounded me on every side. They surrounded me like bees. They blazed like a fire of thorns, but in the name of the Lord I cut them off. I was pushed hard and I was falling, but the Lord helped me. The Lord is my strength and my might and has become my salvation. I thank you that you answered me and became my salvation. I shall not die, but I will live. This is the day the Lord has made, let us rejoice and be glad in it. You are my God and I will give thanks to you. Oh, give thanks to the Lord, for He is good, His steadfast love endures forever! Amen."*

Now if you saw the flow in that Psalm, King David who wrote it, began by giving thanks to the Lord and then he talks about his life. He was surrounded. He was pushed and shoved. There were like bees swarming around him. They are like thorns. He was falling and he cried out to the Lord for help and the Lord answered him and then he could say, "This is the day the Lord has made."

Have you ever had a root canal? Did you ever have a test to take that was just awful? Did you ever go through some horrible personal struggle? In the midst of that experience it is hard for us to cry out, "This is the day the Lord has made," but you know once it is gone and once the pain is over and once that root canal does not hurt anymore, oh it feels so good and that's when you can say, "This is the day the Lord has made." You see, the writer of the 118th Psalm was one day farther away from whatever was bad and one day closer to a place where he could lift up his arms in praise to the Lord. In my world that has a very specific meaning.

You know that Iran has landed troops on the coast of Nicaragua. Iranian Revolutionary Guard Troops landed at a place called Monkey Point, Nicaragua. They marched into the village and they declared to the 600 inhabitants of Monkey Point, Nicaragua that they were going to kick them off their land, spend 350 million dollars to dig a deep water port on the coast of Nicaragua. If they could get jobs, it would be jobs digging ditches and to get a job they had to convert to something called Islam and then they left. That came out in the Wall Street Journal on September 29, 2009, but it actually started December 17, 2007. I saw it in the San

Antonio Express Star, a little short article, but very graphic about the presence of Iranian troops in our backyard.

On December the 18th, I had my tickets to Nicaragua and Dr. Chris Price and I flew down to Managua, flew across to Blue Fields, took a ship down the coast of Nicaragua, ended up in a place called Monkey Point so that we could visit with the villagers and find out how does it feel to have Iranian Revolutionary Guard soldiers come marching into your village and declare that they are going to kick you off your own land. Well, they did not like it. They did not like the idea that they got jobs and had to convert to something called Islam because they are all Christian, and they don't even know what Islam is. We decided we would talk to them about their village in ways that we could help them reconstruct their village and gain some strength in life. The long and short of it is, we built two new churches, we re-did their school, we added uniforms to the children, school supplies, clean water systems, put in sidewalks, we have two baseball teams now, we have a ship that they use to carry supplies, food and people to market and back again to develop their economy, but the neatest thing we did is that we equipped the villagers of Monkey Point with our solar-powered digital Bibles in English, Spanish, and Farsi, the language of Iran.

When the Iranian Revolutionary Troops came back, the courageous Christians of Monkey Point met them with Bibles in hand. They put those Bibles in their hands and said you go listen to this and then come back and talk to us and they kicked them out of the village. Their ambassador went on the radio to say he was displeased with Senior Ben.

Twice I invited the commander of the Iranian Revolutionary Guard to meet me personally to discuss our mutual interest in Monkey Point. I invited him to meet me in the lobby of the Intercontinental Hotel in Managua, Nicaragua on April 23, 2009. I was there at the appointed hour and he did not show up. I began sending letters in Farsi to Akbar Ishmail Pour, the ambassador from Iran to Nicaragua. I invited him to visit me in the United States and that I would go to Iran with him.

When all the fighting started in Tehran, I invited him to defect and come to the United States. I had my envoy, Dr. Chris Price, deliver the letters to the Embassy along with our solar-powered Bibles in Farsi. The ambassador and his staff caught Chris, they took him in the Embassy and they asked about the Bible. He said, "What is what?" He held up the Bible and said, "What do you think it is?" They said, "We think it is a bomb." Chris said, "It's just a Bible." I cannot help but laugh at the image of the Iranian Ambassador and the commanding officer of the Iranian Revolutionary Guard staring at our digital solar-powered Bible and saying you touch it. No, you touch it. No you touch it. I'm not going to touch it. I have an idea, get Jose and let Jose touch the thing. God's word is so powerful it scared our enemies and to me that means we are one day closer to peace.

I left there and I went down to Venezuela. We are on the Manamo River. There were Warao Indians. There were 22,000 of them and less than 200 have ever heard the name of Jesus. Now, Hugo Chavez is the dictator of Venezuela. He has kicked out all the missionaries, but his government gave us written permission to do whatever we wanted to do in the Manamo River basin. Go figure. Our goal was to try to share the gospel with folks who only speak Warao. There is nothing written in their language that helps us out, but we could get *The Jesus Film* in Warao. I ordered copies of it and then realized if we put DVD players down there they have to have electricity and batteries. There is none of that in the jungles of Venezuela. So we worked with a group from Social Circle, Georgia and we created a solar-powered DVD player. We took 10 of these to Venezuela with 10 copies of *The Jesus Film*, along with 10 copies of a movie that I made of that region a year earlier and 10 copies of a film called *Finding Nemo*. They do not have villages along this river. They have family gatherings of several generations. We met with a group of those families and in each location we planted the gospel and they would share that with each other and then put it in their canoes, go down the river and share it with the next family. It was not until the last day of showing this film that an old man stood up and raised his hands and he yelled, "Cristo! I know this story!" Only one man in all the people we met had ever heard the name of Jesus, but now by planting solar-powered DVD players and *The Jesus Film* in their own language, we are bringing the Warao tribe one day closer to knowing Jesus.

I left there and kept heading south and I went to Iguazu Falls, the largest water falls in the world. They are located at the juncture of Argentina, Brazil, and Paraguay. I stayed on the Argentine side and I would cross from Argentina to Brazil, and over to Paraguay to seek a little distance from the folks who live in Ciudad Del Este, Paraguay. You have heard of Hong Kong. You have heard of Miami. Did you know that Ciudad Del Este, Paraguay is the third largest retail zone in the world? Most of us do not know that, but it is because Ciudad Del Este is the home of 25,000 Hamas terrorists. They were planted there from Lebanon 30 years ago on purpose. They send hundreds of millions of dollars back to Hamas and Palestine every year because of drugs, prostitution, illicit weapons, counterfeit goods, and regular retail. It is incredible and they are in our back yard.

There are 25,000 of them. There is one of me and I decided I would go down and see what would happen. "Three" is our administrator and Three got on Google Earth and she searched the city of Ciudad Del Este, Paraguay and she found the main mosque. She told me that mosque was where we would start and I said, "Okay Three, that's great. It's a big city, can you get me a little more information?"

She did a search on Google Earth and she found a street sign and found that the mosque is on Avenue Whatever. So I will go to Avenue Whatever, find the mosque, knock on the door, and who do I want to see? She called me back and said if I could find him, I wanted to meet Mohamed Yusuf Abdullah. Who is that? That is the man who blew up the Israeli Embassy in Buenos Aries, Argentina and killed 12 people. I said, "Okay that works. I'll go there."

So I flew to Argentina and I went from Argentina to Brazil and into Paraguay, I found the mosque, I walked alongside the mosque and walked into the office building attached to the mosque. In the lobby I was confronted by a crowd of men who came pouring out of different shops all dressed in their Hajj robes and they came up to me and in a very demanding voice said, "Who are you? What do you want? Why are you here?"

I obviously had walked into a den of vipers! I looked at the men and said, "I am looking for Mohamed Yusuf Abdullah." The man in my face looked back at me and said, "That is me." He took me to the 19th floor of the apartment building, we went into his apartment, I opened two huge picture windows so I could take photographs of Ciudad Del Este from the 19th floor, and I photographed Mohamed without his knowing it and he got really wired up about the bombing in Argentina, pulled out the business card of the Israeli detective who had interrogated him and got in my face yelling and shouting.

It got so desperate I thought that perhaps one of us was going out the window. I got him calmed down long enough for him to ask me what I wanted and why I was here. I told him the truth. I told him I had family who were dying in the Middle East. She is surrounded by very kind Muslim folks and I have come to say thank you. He said, "You came all the way to Paraguay to say thank you?" I said, "Yes." He said, "Okay, go away and come back in two days." I came back in two days and he had checked me out and said, "Alright, what do you want?" I said, "I want to meet the local Islamic school." He took me to the local Lebanese Islamic school and I spent two days with their headmaster. We talked about the United States. We talked about Lebanon. We talked about Iran. We talked about his hate for our country and our country's apparent hate for Lebanon. He invited me to Lebanon, but said you cannot invite me to the United States because I cannot go. He showed me pictures of his trip to the Hajj. He gave me a Quran and finally said, "What do you want?" I said, "I would like to know how I could help your school." He said, "We have 300 students. We feed 3,000 families. We build clinics and schools across South America. We are very wealthy. We really do not need any help. You could underwrite a scholarship for a child if you would like to." So I did that.

He asked me what else I wanted and I said, "I would like to pair your school with a school in Georgia, would that be possible?" He said, "Sure." He agreed to let me pair his Hamas school with a Christian school in Georgia with the idea that young people in both places would share CDs of music, DVDs of their world, pictures, emails, discussions, and my goal is that perhaps, just perhaps, we could be one day closer to a little understanding between Christian kids in the United States and Islamic kids in Paraguay." Imagine it! I am scheduled to go back this fall, but I have not heard back from them. I don't know if they have changed their mind or if that door is still open. I will let you know.

I left there and I went to the Congo. Oh, I love Congo! We have an orphanage with 30 children who had spent their time living under a tree before we talked about their plight on Christian radio and now they have a home to live in, they have a school, they have a place to eat, and they have clean water. It is just amazing! These kids are good to go. When I got there, there were not 30 children, only about 15. I said, "Oomba, where are the rest of our kids?" Oomba said, "These are children who are orphans of war. That means that their families are not necessarily dead, it means that they lost their families." We have been able to reunite over 20 children with their families. Imagine that. Imagine how it must feel to walk a child home to see their parents who thought perhaps their child was dead and a child who thought perhaps their parents were lost forever. To see them reunited and to see that every day we are one day closer to taking another child home. One day closer to peace. One day closer to knowing Jesus. One day closer to understanding. One day closer to going home.

Okay, how about your world? How are you doing? The economy is still awful. The wars are still raging. Are you worried about a child in your life? Are you suffering financially? Are you worried about our country, or have you got it all pulled together? Is your life scattered across the kitchen floor like the ice that fell out of my freezer? There are two things that I want you to know. Let's go back and look at the Psalm again. He begins by saying, "Give thanks to the Lord for He is good. His steadfast love endures forever." If you noticed, he ends the psalm by saying, "Give thanks to the Lord for He is good. His steadfast love endures forever." Everything in between the beginning and the end of that psalm is what we call life. What I want you to know is that in tough times many of us go to our knees in prayer, nothing happens and we become frustrated with it and we wonder is God even listening and it is because we have forgotten a simple, Biblical principal.

When my son, Adam, went to war for the first time, so many people asked me "what is it like to send your son to war?" I gave the answer then that I would give now; it is actually a question. "What price are we willing to pay for freedom?" I would give that answer very bravely and then I would go home and get in my boat and stick in a CD of music that my son and I made together and I would drive around the lake and listen to the music that my son enjoyed and I would cry and pray that my son would come home safely. In doing this I realized that my son had a better than average chance of getting out of their alive. It was a terrible experience, but he survived. He was a combat infantry platoon leader in the Marine Corps. His first time in battle was the Battle of Fallujah. He started with 42 marines and ended with 25. He lost three, I think, and the rest were wounded, but my son came home. In considering that, you know what went through my mind? My son came home okay. How did God feel when our Heavenly Father knew that He was sending His Only Son to die on the cross for you and for me? When we get in hard times we get on our knees and we do not remember to say "Thank you Jesus for the sacrifice that you made for me." Instead we get on our knees and in hard times we beg God to give us a pony. Oh God, give me a better job. Oh God, let me get along with my family. Oh God, let my children be okay. Oh God, give me more money. Give me, give me, give me, and we never remember to say thank you and then we wonder why God does not seem to respond. This is such a simple, Biblical principal that when we come into the presence of the Lord begin and end everything you do just as the writer of the 118th Psalm. "Give thanks to the Lord for He is good. His steadfast love endures forever." You have heard me say it before, in difficult times when I feel a bout of pessimism coming over me, instead of allowing it to rock my world, instead right out loud I say, "Thank you Jesus." Thank you Jesus. Thank you Jesus and I keep saying those words over and over again, until my praises are louder than my pessimism and then my pessimism goes away.

When you come into the presence of the Lord, first of all, give thanks to God that opens the channel to His heart, thanksgiving opens God's heart to you and then share your needs after that and then give thanks again for God's love and His response to your needs.

If you could see me now, I'm reaching into my pocket and I am pulling out my iPhone. I answer the iPhone and I say, "Hello. Oh hey Jesus, how are you? Oh yeah, I'm fine. No, I'm in church, and I'm preaching right now. Oh yea, of course you knew that. Yes, I'm going to tell them that. No, Lord that wasn't me, well it was me last night. I'm sorry, I confess. No, it won't happen again. I promise Lord, I will do my best. Yes. Okay Lord. Yes, I'll be sure to tell them. Thank you Jesus. I mean Thank You Lord. Alright, talk to you later." Now, I'm going to hold up my phone and show it to you. What is this? It's an iPhone. How many of you have one of these? Raise your hands. That's cool. You know, what do we do when we buy an iPhone? It's incredible. The first thing we do is buy a case to put it in to protect it. What do we do at night? Oh, we take our phone and plug it in and give it a chance to recharge. When it rings, what do we do? Well, you just saw me in your pulpit. Apparently, wherever we are, we stop and we answer our iPhone. We protect them. Have you ever left your iPhone at home? Oh…. have you ever left it somewhere and you thought you had lost it? How did you feel? Here's what I want you to know today.

I would like you to know that God wants us to first of all be thankful. Secondly, I want you to know that God wants us to treat each other as well as we treat our iPhones. Protect those you love. Give them a chance to recharge. Take them with you wherever you go. Whether it is in your heart or physically. Take them with you wherever you go. When they call, answer. When they speak, listen. Cherish the people you love, more than your iPhone. In fact, if you have the courage, sometime tonight sit down with the people you love and say "I love you more than I love my iPhone." For that I am grateful. I hope you are too. God bless you. Stay strong and God bless America.

Prepared to Praise

Acts 16:6-10

> *"They passed through the Phrygian and Galatian region, having been forbidden by the Holy Spirit to speak the word in Asia; and after they came to Mysia, they were trying to go into Bithynia, and the Spirit of Jesus did not permit them; and passing by Mysia, they came down to Troas. A vision appeared to Paul in the night: a man of Macedonia was standing and appealing to him, and saying, 'Come over to Macedonia and help us.' When he had seen the vision, immediately we sought to go into Macedonia, concluding that God had called us to preach the gospel to them."*

In your mind, I want you to go to Northeastern Guatemala. It is late in the day, and I'm in your basic mud hut with a thatched roof. There is one light bulb hanging down and there is a ceiling fan. Now, I did not know this, but at exactly 11:00 at night somebody turns off the generator. I could hear it in the distance go "pop, pop, pop, haaaa." All of a sudden it got dark. Even in the darkness I could look up and I could see the ceiling fan as it ground to a halt and it stopped and the heat just settled over me like a big blanket.

Well, I was ready for it. I got out of bed and I took a little towel and I dipped it in the wash basin, rung out the towel, put it over my head, climbed back in bed, and I fell sound asleep. Now, I was just getting into a good sleep when the

Lord spoke to me and said, "Wake up. Something is wrong." I did not move a muscle. I started listening in case someone was coming in the window or trying to open the door. Out one direction I could hear crickets…that was good. In another direction I could hear an owl…that was also good. I listened in another direction and could hear some lizards that make sort of an odd sound…that was all wonderful. It meant no one was trying to open the door. It further meant whatever was wrong was already in the hut with me!

I reached over and got my flashlight. My first thought was there was a huge snake in the rafters and I was about to become dinner. I turned on the flashlight, I went across the rafters and there was nothing there. I went down one side of the bed, nothing there. I shined the light down another side of the bed, nothing there. Whatever was wrong had to be right down at the foot of the bed. I put the flashlight under my chin and I lifted myself as slowly as I could just in time to see an ugly creature climbing over my feet right towards me.

I reached over the side of the bed, took the metal cup I travel with, poured the water out, reached over and got one of my sandals, and I decided I would scoop the scorpion into the cup. I put the flashlight in my mouth, I sat up, and I hit the scorpion with my shoe! Have you ever hit a scorpion with a shoe? They don't do a thing. They just sit there. I hit him again and all he did was hunker down and raise his tail. That undid me! The third time I swatted him really hard, I rolled him over, and I pushed him into the cup. I then put the sandal on top of the cup, set it down on the floor and climbed back in the bed. As I was falling back asleep, I just could not be amazed that the Lord went to all that trouble to wake me up in the jungles of Guatemala.

I was a little impressed that I had listened when God tried to wake me up. I could not help but wonder if that scorpion could lift the sandal up off the cup. This was not Paul and Silas' problem at all in our text today. Paul and Silas listened to the Lord like it was an everyday occurrence. Do you remember what it said? The Lord said, "Don't go here." So they didn't. "Don't speak over here," so they didn't. So the Lord said, "Come on to Macedonia" and immediately they packed their bags and away they went. Don't you wish we listened like that? I mean just listened to each other, much less to the Lord.

I have two boys. One of them is named Benjamin. When Benjamin was 18, I took him to a war in southern Mexico, a guerrilla war, in an area called Chiapas. We went there looking for a way to help find peace along a river called the Agua Azul. It is literally a bright, blue river that comes crashing down out of the Jungle Mountains. It is just breathtaking.

We went with Erma Garcia De LaToya, a Presbyterian missionary. When we were at the bottom of the river, people were bathing and doing their laundry. We climbed off into the jungle and as we continued to follow the river, we saw fewer and fewer people. However, the people we saw all said the same thing, "You don't need to be here. This area is controlled by the guerrillas. You don't need to be here. Why don't you turn around and go back?" We did not listen. We kept going.

The next people we saw were a little more adamant. "You need to turn around and go back." The next people said, "This is not good. You don't belong here, go away." Erma looked at us and she said, "Do you know, I was actually born about three miles farther up this river? Would you like to see where I was raised as a little girl?" Benjamin was 18 and had never been in a situation like this. I looked at Benjamin and said, "Benjamin, what do you want to do?" He said, "Let's go Dad." I said, "Okay, here are the rules. You will stay behind me. If we run into anybody, you are not to say a word. You are not to make eye contact. You are not to move. Do you understand that?" I want you to get a clear picture. We were in shorts, boots, and were carrying great big backpacks with all of our gear. We were climbing over boulders alongside this jungle river. After a while, you really start concentrating on not banging your knees up on the rocks and not falling down and quite honestly you quit paying attention. That's what happened to us.

We walked for hours, and it just sort of became monotonous. I have to admit that I was not paying attention and all of a sudden right in front of us, two men appeared on the jungle path and it scared our missionary so desperately that she jumped.

Now you've done that before, haven't you? Go ahead and shake your head. It might not have been gorillas in the mist, but you've done that. Somebody told you, "don't you go there" and you went. Don't you eat that, don't you smoke that, don't you touch that, but you did it anyway. You got caught and what did you do? Don't we all just jump in disbelief? We got caught.

Immediately Erma started talking and she said when she was a little girl she was raised on the other side of that river. "All of this land used to belong to my grandfather. I bathed in this river until I was 15 years old," Erma continued. One of the men walked up to your missionary, put his hands on her shoulder, looked her in the eye and said, "I used to work for your grandfather. It is okay, you are safe. You are with family."

Paul was with family. Paul was with God's family and the Lord said to Paul, don't go there, so he did not. Do not speak here, so he does not. And because Paul was obedient, God gave him a vision and in the vision Paul was instructed to go to Macedonia so and he and his companions were then on their way. There needs to come a point in all of our lives, and I pray that today is that day when you will come forward and say, "Lord give me something to taste, touch, and feel to renew my relationship with you. Lord today is the day when I can say I will give back to you so that the work here continues." This is the day when we need to listen to what God wants us to do with our lives. For those of us with *Rivers of the World* (ROW), it meant "go back to the Congo." For Paul, it meant, "Go to Macedonia."

To get to the Democratic Republic of the Congo (DRC), we had to fly for three days, departing from Atlanta and arriving just in the middle of the country. We landed in Kananga and then we took a bush plane the last 300 miles and landed in the jungle. Well, the bush plane crashed. Nobody was hurt, but we were out a plane. We had been traveling for three days. It was five in the afternoon and to get further up country where we needed to go, we had to pile into the back of pickup trucks. So from 5 p.m. until 5 a.m. the next morning, we drove across the DRC hanging onto the sides of the trucks.

After sleeping for two hours on a concrete floor of an abandoned building, we dragged everything down to the river where there was one dug-out canoe waiting for us. For the next nine hours, we traveled up the Lubi River until we arrived at our river, the Sankuru, where we picked up our staff and kept going north until it was dark; we had been up 36 hours. We set up our tents on a sandbar. To take a bath, you have to walk off into the river and, considering how we were feeling, you just hope something eats you and gets it over with.

I came back to the tent, pulled back my rain fly, climbed in and I lay down. I looked up at the stars, thinking, "Lord I have sand in my teeth, sand in my hair, sand in my ears, I am 40-something years old, is this it? Is this what you want out of my life?" You know what I thought about next? I thought about Paul. Paul was obedient to go. He went to Macedonia. We try to be obedient and sometimes we end up going to the Congo. You know what happened to Paul in Macedonia? He got thrown in jail. Paul was in the slammer. Ben is on the sandbar. What is the difference? If you read the Book, the Book will tell you that Paul and Silas were singing hymns and praising God. I thought, "You know Lord, we're Presbyterian. We don't do that very well."

How many of you were in Sunday School this morning? You saw a music video of the song that Andrae Crouch wrote for us. I am just thrilled by the whole process. Babbie

Mason, a wonderful Christian artist, was the lead singer for the song. To make that happen, I went to Andrae's church in the barrios of LA. His church is different from our church. There are 19 microphones across the front and a large area for an orchestra. Stevie Wonder and Aretha Franklin will drop by just to sing a song on the way to church somewhere. It is quite an experience. In between songs people will get up, come down to the microphones, and they will look at the congregation and say things like, "I've been set free from poverty. I got a job!" The church will then all yell, "Thank you Jesus!" And the next person will come up and say, "I'm clean! I've been set free from drugs." The church will yell, "Thank you Jesus!"

Following the testimonies, the congregation sings a song. The praises go up, the blessings come down. The praises go up, the blessings come down. With this reminder, on the sand bar, I started saying, "Lord, I've got sand in my teeth. Thank you Jesus! It means I don't have to brush my teeth tonight. Lord, something is probably going to drag me off in the river and eat me tonight. Thank you Jesus! I hope I taste bad. Lord, I have sand in my hair. Thank you Jesus! That means I don't need shampoo. Thank you Jesus!"

Now let me ask you something. I have spent half my life in a tent. That is not at all what I thought my life would be. How about you? Right this very second, right now, look at your life. Is this where you thought you would be right now? Is it just great? You are making so much money you are probably going to underwrite the whole church budget all on your own. You and your spouse are just getting closer every day. You have the best grandbabies in the whole wide world, don't you? Hmmm. Or do you have grandchildren driving you nuts? Do you have parents driving you up the wall? Things are not working at home or at work or at school, are they?

Let's do a little litany before we get ready for communion. I am going to say something and you are going to answer back, "thank you Jesus!" but do it like you mean it. Let's try this. Lord, life is great! "Thank you Jesus!" the congregation replied. Now, the choir did okay but y'all sounded like you just ordered an apple pie from Jesus at McDonald's. Yes, Lord I'll have that apple pie, thank you Jesus. Let's try this one more time. Lord, life is great! "Thank you Jesus!" shouted the congregation. Lord, my wife and I are so happy that Dr. Ruth is calling me for advice. "Thank you Jesus!" the congregation shouted. Lord, I've got the best kids in the whole world! "Thank you Jesus!" the congregation said loudly. Lord, I am so proud of my grandbabies! "Thank you Jesus!" said the congregation. Lord, I am old and alone! Don't get quiet on me. Lord, I am old and alone. "Thank you Jesus," said the congregation with much less enthusiasm. Come on now, stay with me. Lord, I don't know how I'm going to pay my bills. "Thank you Jesus," the congregation said. Lord, I'm scared. "Thank you Jesus," everyone replied. But I know you're the Lord. "Thank you Jesus," said the congregation. And everything's going to be all right. "Thank you Jesus," recited the congregation.

I did that on that sandbar. I was scared to death but I kept saying "thank you Jesus" until I started laughing and until I fell asleep. The next day we worshipped with about 800 people, and I didn't have a clue what they were saying, but we had a ball. We ministered by treating people with river blindness, giving away Bibles in French, and immunizing a bunch of their children against childhood diseases. I came back to that sandbar and it felt a whole lot more like home. I learned something. I learned that if we give the Lord a chance, He will tell you what to say, what not to say, where to go, and where not to go. If we are just obedient to God, He will give us a vision for our lives and He will give us the ability to complete that vision. I learned above everything else, if we lift our praises up, we are showered with blessings and all I can say to that is, "thank you Jesus!"

Look, I know some of you are about to give an offering to your church. God bless you for it, but consider doubling it, and have some faith. I know that some of you are preparing to come to the Lord's Table to finally let go of something, to pick something up or take a step in your life. That is what this is all about. You are safe to take that step. But I also know that this afternoon some of you are going to pick back up those things you offered to God. Now, next Sunday when Tom gets here, if he says something you really like, you let out a good "thank you Jesus!" and let me know what happens. God bless you.

> *Heavenly, Father, I ask that you give to me ears that can hear you more clearly. Grant me eyes that can see your presence more in my life. Above all else, I ask that you give to me more of a willing and obedient heart to follow after you. When you instruct me to go somewhere, may I not hesitate? When you impress upon me to speak, may I do so immediately. When you nudge me to keep quiet,*

may I listen? Keep my life completely in tune with your will, I pray. Thank you, Jesus that you have given to me the Holy Spirit to be my guide and to keep me in the very center of your will. I pray these things in your name, Jesus, amen.

Rejoice and Be Glad

"Now when John heard in prison about the deeds of the Christ, he sent word by his disciples and said to Him, "Are You He who is to come, or shall we look for another?" And Jesus answered them, "Go and tell John what you hear and see; the blind receive their sight and the lame walk, lepers are cleansed and the deaf hear, and the dead are raised up and the poor have good news preached to them. And blessed is he who takes no offense at me."
Matthew 11: 2-6 (RSV)

Changing the world for Christ requires much more than words. If we go by our words alone, we can often be mistaken. As one who travels the Church, I sometimes arrive a little early to have a chance to visit with pastors. It is important to learn the life of the Church and to stay in touch with my colleagues who serve on the front lines in pulpits across the United States.

Brother Taylor knew that I was coming by a little early. I was amazed that he was not in his office when I appeared. His secretary was gone for the afternoon, so I decided to just walk around the Church and see if perhaps he was studying in the library, or another part of the building. I walked across the first floor of the education wing and looked in the adult Sunday school classes. No sign of Brother Taylor. I found the library, but it was empty as well. The Fellowship Hall had been set for our dinner meeting, and the nursery lights had been left on. As I walked across the Fellowship

Hall towards the nursery, I heard a strange sound. "Thump, thump!" I wondered if they had rabbits in the children's area. Before I could move on to my next thought, I heard the sound of someone falling to the floor. Roaring laughter erupted in the nursery. I peered into the children's room and rolling on the floor was Brother Taylor. Tears streaming down his cheeks, he was laughing so hard he was having difficult time breathing. I helped him up, dusted him off, and gave him a hug.

"Well, Brother Taylor, tell me what in the world is going on!" I said curiously. Still breathing hard and trying to regain his composure, Brother Taylor sat down on one of the teacher's chairs and responded, "Well, Ben, I knew you were coming today. I knew that you would talk to us about stewardship and service and serving on the mission field, and I wanted to be ready for you. I decided it would be a good idea to go through every level of the church and do a slight review of our stewardship. I wanted to find out how we were using all that God has given us. I decided to start in the nursery. I have uncovered something that is very disturbing." With that, he got quiet and looked more serious. I pulled up my chair next to him and spoke in quiet terms, "Tell me about it Brother."

"It seems that we have a large number of very young children in our congregation. When they come to church on Sunday mornings, they come wearing those cute little frilly britches over their diapers. When they come into the nursery, the nursery workers take the frilly britches off of them and cover their diapers with the basic plastic pants with three snaps up on either side. That way, they can play in the nursery without getting their little frilly britches all dirty. I have uncovered something that is shocking. It seems that inadvertently, several of our young couples have been carrying off our plastic pants! I am down to six pairs of plastic britches!" I could see at this point, that Brother Taylor was getting serious. Rather than let him lose the mood, I allowed him to continue to his tale of woe. "I came up with a way to handle the problem. I decided that I would take a rubber stamp and stamp right on the bottom of every pair of plastic pants 'First Presbyterian Church,' right there on the bottom of those britches, I had stamped 'For Deposit Only'!" We laughed until we cried. However, the point it was obvious, using the wrong words can sometimes get you into trouble!

Now I want you to imagine John's predicament in our text. John is in prison. He is stuck in some Roman jail cell, and yet the people around him change constantly. Guards come and go. Inmates come and go. But John is stuck in jail. As the guards and inmates cross the path of John's life, they undoubtedly brought with them stories of this man Jesus. Can't you just imagine it? "I heard He gave sight to a blind man." "Yes and I heard He fed 5,000 people!" "Is it true that He can walk on water and raise the dead?" How in the world did John feel? Unable to get to the Lord, and yet hearing only bits and pieces about His ministry. Again, you have probably experienced this in your own life. You are traveling from point A to point B, and finally something worthwhile comes on the radio. Perhaps they are announcing football scores, and you are finally going to hear if UNC beat North Carolina State. Just as the announcer reads your particular score, you pass under a tunnel or alongside a very loud truck. You fail to hear what Paul Harvey so aptly calls "the rest of the story." That is so frustrating!

John must have felt this sense of frustration and that is why he sent his disciples to ask one of the most important question in history to Jesus, "Are you He who is to come, or shall we look for another?"

Why in the world did Jesus not take this opportunity and settle a lot of questions for us all? Why did He not simply say to the disciples of John, "Go and tell John that I am the Messiah?" That would have settled it. John would have had his questions answered, and could have rested in jail peacefully. But would he? Would John have simply accepted the Messiahship of Christ and let it go at that? Of course not. John would have had an Old Testament understanding of the Messiah. He probably would have expected Jesus to become a great military ruler, to ride into town with legions of soldiers, and kick the Romans out of town. He might have expected Jesus to open the doors of the jail, set John free and make him a high-ranking official in the new order of things. That would have been tragically limiting for such a limitless God.

Instead of such a blunt response, Jesus very wisely tells the disciples of John to relay the message that says basically, "Go and tell John what you see as well as what you hear. The blind receive their sight, the lame walk, the deaf hear, the dead are raised up, and the poor have good news preached to them." It appears that Jesus was interested in having John understand not only His words, but His deeds as well. Then John could draw his own conclusion concerning the Messiahship of Jesus.

As I travel the world on behalf of Presbyterian medical missions, I always pray for the Lord to allow me to experience something that I can carry back to the Church as words of hope and encouragement. I believe that Christians will respond to needs more appropriately if they understand that the work of the Lord goes beyond our words to our deeds as well.

On a particular trip to Zaire, I was joined by two other missionaries on a short drive to the Chutes. The Chutes is actually a rapidly moving portion of the Lube River in Zaire. The belief is that Hippos and Crocodiles do not particularly take to fast moving water. If the water is rough and rapid, you have a better that 50-50 chance of being able to get into the river, bathe and get back out, without becoming someone's lunch. We were heading for an afternoon at the river!

The roads in this part of Zaire are very much like country roads in the South, basically sand and rough; they seem to go on forever. I was driving a Toyota Land Cruiser at the time. It was late in the afternoon. Approximately 50 yards ahead of me someone rolled across the road. By her dress, I could tell it was a woman. It appeared that she was having a convulsion or a seizure of some type, so I sped the Land Cruiser up to be of assistance. Arriving at her side, I rolled down the window to discover that this woman was in fact thrashing in the African dirt. Screaming at the top of her lungs and wailing as if she were in great pain, I was convinced that something horrible had happened to her. As we prepared to get out of the truck, someone came up and explained to us that there must have been a death in her family, and she was simply grieving. The people of Africa are beautifully expressive. When a baby is born, the women of a village will generally escort the mother and child home. As they walk back to their village, they engage themselves in dancing, music, and loud chanting and clapping. Songs of celebration to God for a new birth are often the music for the rest of the day! As in birth, so in death, the people of Zaire express their emotions openly.

In light of this situation, we did what any of us would do, we looked at the woman and said, "I wish there was something I could do"–and we drove off.

You have experienced this before. You have had an argument with your spouse. You have said something a little too strongly to your children. Perhaps you have reprimanded someone with whom you work. You do your best to walk away from the situation, but find that your heartstrings are being tugged. You simply go back to that person for some sort of resolution and reconciliation. As I continued to drive down the dusty African road, I felt that woman tugging at my heart. I must confess I drove for almost a mile before I stopped, "I have to go back. I cannot leave that woman rolling in the dirt," I said. "Ben, what are you going to do? Your Tshiluba is awful and your French is an embarrassment to us all. What are you going to do?" the missionaries responded. "I do not know, but I am not going to leave that woman in the dirt. I am going back," I answered.

I turned the truck around and was relieved to find the woman still grieving by the side of the road. I did not know if this woman was a Christian or one who practiced witchcraft and animism. As I stepped out of the truck, I decided I want her to know who I was and who I serve. I sat beside her in the dirt. She appeared to be 70 or 80 years old – the oldest woman I have ever seen in Africa. I put my arms around her and she immediately placed her head upon my chest and sobbed. In Tshiluba the word for woman is "Baba." I gently rocked the woman back and forth in my arms and said quietly, "Oh Baba I am so sorry, I am so sorry." At this point she needed to know who I served. I whispered into her ear "Jesu Ydi Mukelenge" (translation: Jesus is Lord).

Immediately she quit crying. She wiped the tears and dust from her face, stood slowly, straightened her dress and took my hand. She began leading me down the dusty road. I looked to my friends in the Land Cruiser, and said, "Follow me. I guess we are going for a walk." As they prepared to start the Land Cruiser and follow me, a lady came out of the local village and explained to us that this woman's grandson had died. We now understood the reason for her grief.

As we walked down the road together, I spoke out loud in English to the Lord, "Lord, this woman cannot understand a word I am saying. I do not speak enough French to talk to her and I surely do not speak enough Tshiluba. Lord, I am going to talk to this woman in English, and I want you to translate for me. Thank You Lord. Amen." Before I could begin sharing my heart with this dear lady, I learned in the most beautiful way that she was in fact a Christian. As we walked through a local village, the little children would come right to the edge of the road, wave to the lady and in their most cheerful voice, say, "Alleluia!" She would answer by slowly waving her hand back to the children and nodding with a smile while responding "Amen." Holding her hand and speaking as gently as possible, I looked at her and said "You know, I have two little boys. I have Benjamin who is this big (I held my hand 4 feet off the ground) and I have Adam who is this big (and I held my hand approximately 3 feet off the ground). If something happened to one of them, I just don't know what I would do. I want you to know that I am so sorry for the death in your family." I looked at her silently, and learned that she understood! Slowly she raised her right hand almost to my shoulder and spoke. Then in slow succession she lowered her hand a little at a time as she told me about the members of her family. She did just fine until she got to the smallest member of the family and then she broke down and cried on my shoulder.

Her crying drew the attention of a local villager. He came up to us speaking French, explaining to me that the woman's grandson had died that morning. He was four years old and had starved to death. He had not been placed in the Earth yet and she wanted me to come to their village. Of course, I agreed.

The missionaries continued to follow us in the truck. We turned off the main road and wound our way through the tall field grass that led to a neighboring village. As we approached their home, it became obvious that there were other adults inside the hut grieving. You could hear their screams and wails from a great distance. The village consisted of ten or twelve round mud huts with thatched roofs. A small opening approximately 3 feet high and 2 feet wide represented the only entrance into a hut. The inside of a Zairian hut is very dark and very cold. I stooped as low as I could to ease my way into the hut.

As my eyes adjusted to the darkness, I realized that there were four or five adults in the hut with me. Some sat against the wall of the hut and found that in the middle of the rooms was the little boy. He was dressed in his best clothes. His hair was gray, his skin was wrinkled, and his little arms were folded across his chest. His body had been placed on a small mat of woven reeds. As the people in the hut became aware of my presence, they slowly ceased their grieving and looked at me instead.

There was really nothing to say. On my knees, I moved slowly toward the little boy's body. I put my hands upon his chest and prayed. I prayed in English, and the others around me prayed in French and Tshiluba. We formed a circle around the little boy and held hands. I said the words to the children's song, "Jesus Loves Me" in Tshiluba. They translate so very beautifully, "Yes we were happy when Jesus came into our lives." We cried. We put our arms around each other's shoulders and tried to console each other. We sat silent and motionless for what seemed like hours.

Finally, it became apparent that it was time for me to go. I left the hut and stood in the brilliance of the afternoon sunset. The missionaries with me hugged me and we walked quietly to the truck. As I opened the door to get inside, the father of the little boy appeared. Through an interpreter, he asked if I would come back the next day and help to bury their child. I agreed and we returned to the hospital.

As I sat on my bed in the guesthouse, I felt the feelings I always feel in times of tragedy. Again, I found myself feeling nauseated and angry. I felt fat and helpless. I felt frustrated and so alone. This time, a new question came to my mind. What is the good that can come out of this experience? What is there that has happened today that I can share with the Church in America? Oh Lord, what is the good of a little boy's death?

After much thought and prayer, it was apparent to me that there was nothing good about a little child dying, but there is something to be learned. You see, when that family had the rug pulled out from under their lives and when that family had their hearts broken, it was not the witch doctor that came to care – he does not. It was not the Army of the Dictator who came bringing food and blankets – because they did not care. It was not the Red Cross who showed up with coffee, donuts, and volunteers – they do not exist in that part of the world. No, when that family's life was so needlessly destroyed by a little boy's death, you and the Church were there. You were the ones who got down on your knees and climbed into their hut. You were the ones who cried with that family, you were the ones who prayed with that family, you were the ones who did all those things, but you did even more. You see, you were the ones who will see to it that doctors are sent to the village, you are the ones who will see to it that food and nutritionists go to that village, you are the ones who will send evangelists to that village, you are the ones who will see to it that no one ever starves to death in that village again, and you have the right to be proud of that! You have the right to rejoice that our Lord is using our Church to make a difference around this world one village at a time. You have a right to rejoice and be glad.

Now, that speaks to the Church. However, you remember that one of my primary axioms in life is that God's word never lets us off the hook as individuals. The last verse in this text speaks to us as individuals. As you recall, Jesus says, "Blessed are you if you take no offense at me." The meaning of this verse revolves around two words, blessed and offense. The Greek word for offend is *scandalitzomai*. It has very ancient origins, probably from Sanskrit. Originally, the word was used to describe someone being thrown against one wall, snatched up and thrown across a room and into another wall. Its meaning evolved to be descriptive of an animal that has fallen into a trap and become impaled on a stick. In many paraphrased versions of the Scriptures, blessed is paraphrased as happy. I personally believe there is nothing farther from the truth. To be blessed is not at all to be happy. There are some of you reading these words now who do things that make you "happy" that you cannot tell me about. No, to be blessed is to experience the joy of participating with God in an act of salvation or healing. Let me describe that joy for you.

A few years ago, I spoke to a conference of American military personnel in England. It was an exciting spiritual event that exposed me to some of the most wonderful Christians I have ever met. While there, one of the speakers was Professor Percival Thistlewhait, a small and gentle man; he was very excited and wanted to share a story with me. Professor Thistlewhait told me that he had never been married and I told him that I could see why! Nevertheless, he shared that each afternoon the children in his neighborhood enjoyed being outside, running, playing, and making the general noise of little children. He also shared that every afternoon the mothers of the neighborhood had virtually 'had it' with their children! Let us let Professor Thistlewhait tell the story from here, as it were, on one afternoon, a dear Mrs. Wilson came out yelling and screaming at her children. I enjoyed going to Mrs. Wilson and saying 'Now tsk, tsk, Mrs. Wilson. Let's just let the children be children,' and I would go back inside and feel very proud of myself. As it were, I had to redo my driveway. I spent the entire day getting the cement just so, and then retired for my tea. As you can well imagine, the children came and were playing and writing in the fresh cement. I lost it! I ran outside and found myself berating the little children, when along comes Mrs. Wilson! 'Tsk, tsk, Professor, now let us just let the children be children!' The woman had me! Thank heaven for my wit! I looked the woman right in the eye and said, 'Mrs. Wilson, I love your children in the abstract, but not in the concrete!'

Do you want to experience a joy that goes beyond any form of happiness you have ever known? Do you want to experience the joy of putting your hand in God's hand and participating in changing the world? If so, then I want you to recognize something.

I want you to recognize that just as the disciples of John came to Jesus, so do the people of your world look to you asking, "Do you represent any hope for me or should I go somewhere else?" Recognize that you are surrounded by people who are held in various sorts of prisons just as honestly as John the Baptist. They are held back by chains of depression or guilt. They are blind of any vision. Some are deaf to any good news. Some are socially outcast. Some are popping with potential. Some lack nothing more than the simple invitation to receive Jesus Christ as Lord and Savior of their lives. All it takes is for us to recognize that we are surrounded by such people who seek discretion and purpose. They long and hunger to know if the things that you do and the things that you do not do, represent Jesus Christ. Do you want to experience the joy of the Lord? Then let me urge you to find a "concrete" way to open your arms to those around you, and proclaim with all your heart, "Jesu Udi Mukelenge" – Jesus Christ is Lord.

The Requirements of Love
1 John 5:1-5

"Everyone who believes that Jesus is the Christ has been born of God. And everyone who loves the parent, loves the child.

By this we know that we love children of God, when we love God and obey His commandments.

The love of God is this, that we obey His commandments. And His commandments are not burdensome.

For whatever is born of God conquers the world; and this is the victory that conquers the world, our faith.

Who is it that conquers the world, but the one who believes that Jesus is the Son of God?"

Amen.

The Apostle John wrote the fourth gospel named after him. He wrote it to reveal to us throughout the ages that Jesus Christ is the Messiah, the Son of God. He follows it by writing the Epistles—First, Second, and Third John. They were specifically given to show you and me how to live our lives. The requirements of love are a tough topic.

If you will look at the text in the verse that follows, he writes very simply the commandment that we have from God.

God's only commandment is that we love one another in Jesus Christ. That sounds simple enough, doesn't it? He goes on to say that this commandment is not burdensome. Literally the word means a crushing weight as if you took a great and heavy stone and dropped it on somebody.

You have known me long enough to know that I believe that this is the word of God, period. But that does not mean that I have to agree with it all the time. And I cannot wait to meet John someday because I want to ask him why he said that. He said that loving somebody is not burdensome, it is not a difficult task.

Well, I don't know you, but I think that John didn't know three of us. You can ask my wife, loving me is not always an easy task. I can promise you that. John didn't know me. John didn't know you. And I bet that loving you is not always an easy task, is it? Well, let me ask in another way. Is it always easy for you to love the person that is sitting next to you?

I don't want to start a fight in my house, not today. And I tell you what else, John did not know Leroy. I have got to tell you, I don't even like Leroy! But I have known him for going on 14 years.

Leroy is my barber. He is not a hair stylist; he is a barber. He makes that very clear to you. I go to Leroy for one reason. When you have as much hair as I do, you don't want to spend much money getting it cut and Leroy is cheap! When you sit down in the chair he puts the apron on you and pulls it over your neck. He made it very clear to me if I wanted to ever talk, I could go down the street and pay $15 and get my hair cut or I could sit there and shut up and he would cut my hair. He is absolutely one of the rudest, most anti-social people I have met in my life, but I continue to go to him and get my hair cut. Not a word is ever said. It is really quite a strange experience.

You have got to add up all these years of going there to really feel the impact of what it was like the day I walked in, sat down, and he put that little apron over me and he actually said, "How are you doing?" I thought, uhhhhh…. He's come to the Lord or something. I don't know what has happened here. I said, "I'm fine, how are you doing?" I mean it was scary. I thought maybe he kind of lost it. Maybe he was going to kill me right there in the chair. I didn't know. He said, "I'm fine. I am getting ready to go fishing." That's more than that man has said to me in 14 years! Something's up! I said, "Well good. Where are you going?" And Leroy began to tell me that he was soon to leave for Florida to go fishing with his best friend, and it would probably be the last time he ever went fishing with his best friend because Leroy's best friend was dying of cancer. It would probably be the last time they ever got to fish together.

As Leroy started talking, a couple of things dawned on me. The first was that obviously this man loved his buddy very deeply. And this was probably the best friend he ever had. He's having a tough time with the fact that his friend is dying and there is nothing he can do about it. I was touched by that. And at the same time, the other half was grabbed and twisted with fear as it dawned on me that the only way Leroy could talk to me was if he was doing something with his hands.

Am I Ever Going to Get Out of Here?

Leroy wanted to talk a long time, and if he was going to talk a long time, he would cut every hair on my head at least twice. I had another option.

I could take off the little apron and get up and move to the next chair and say, "Well, Leroy, tell me how you feel?" Good pastoral stuff, but Leroy would have shut right up, wouldn't he? Or I could sit there and know that this man would cut every hair on my head off, but at least he would pour his heart out to me.

Let me tell you what I learned that day. I learned that one of the toughest requirements of love is that sometimes we just have to sit there and take it. I came home bald headed and my family howled because it looked like I had just enlisted in the Marines. But, by golly, my buddy got to pour his heart out to me. Isn't that the way it is?

Have you ever felt like? Have you ever felt like you wanted to corral the people you love, slam the door behind you, and just keep going? Have you ever felt like that? Have you ever felt that way about people at work? I have had it with this thing, and I am stomping out of here and that is it! Elders...have you ever felt that way about the church? Sometimes love means we just have to sit there and take it. Doesn't it?

Well, if you will look at the text, this is a very powerful passage. He says, "Whoever is born of God, conquers the world." This is the victory that conquers the world or our faith! Faith is the thing that enables us to keep going in life.

I woke up to a horrible storm going on in Jackson. Charlie and I knew we had to get over here anyway. It is faith that says in the mornings, "Lord, I choose to believe you are going to look after me. I am going to go on through this day. I am going to get in the car, and we are going to head on over there, storm or no storm. Lord, you look after us."

That's faith by choice, isn't it? We all have that. We choose to believe the Lord will carry us through the elevator during the day. We choose to believe that the Lord is going to watch after us. But it is those times when life has to be lived with only a faith that is forced upon us that it really gets to the cutting edge, isn't it?

Last April there was a terrible tidal surge in the southern part of Bangladesh. In a matter of hours, hundreds of thousands of people were literally swept away to their deaths. Maybe you remember on TV the helicopters that flew along. The Bengali has one helicopter for the whole nation, and their helicopter flew along the coast, along the Chittagong area. It showed pictures of thousands of animals and people who had been lost in the tide.

When I see things like that around the world, it is overwhelming and I cannot comprehend a disaster like that.

After that disaster, I finally got a letter from our friends in Bangladesh. They said that a hundred and thirty-eight thousand people died in that tidal wave. That is hard to imagine. It still did not make a lot of sense until they brought it closer to home.

Bangladesh is a Muslim country. That means if you are a Christian, you are isolated from the rest of the community. Your family may try to kill you. They will definitely disown you and run you out of the village and most of the Christians who work with us Presbyterians, work with us in western Bangladesh, but they come from northeast. They had to leave their families hundreds of miles away with no hope of ever coming home. They fled across Bangladesh and they live and in our small Christian community.

Two Christians who lived on the coast by the storm had written to your missionaries. One had no idea the storm was coming. In an attempt to save his life, this man saw the flood and the tidal surge coming, and he did the only thing he could do. He climbed onto the roof of his house. By now the storm was blowing so hard things are flying through the air. He was knocked unconscious.

He came to hours later. He survived. When he came to, he was still on the roof of his house, but the roof of his house was 15 miles from where he had been knocked unconscious. Somehow, his roof was picked up and carried that far, yet he survived.

How many of you have daughters? I have two boys. To be rich in Bangladesh is not to own a vehicle or to have electricity or a television. To be rich is to own a radio.

The second family my friends told me about are wealthy Christians in south Bangladesh—they owned a radio. The good news is that it entertains. The bad news is that they knew the storm was coming and there was nothing they could do about it. You cannot out run the monsoons in Bangladesh. The land is so flat, you can literally see for miles and miles and miles. And the sky one minute will be beautiful and bright blue and then when the monsoons blow up instantly. It is as if it is rolling toward you. These huge black clouds come rolling like their chasing you. You cannot get away.

This man heard on the radio that a tidal surge was coming from below and that the storm's coming from above and he could not escape. He has a wife and five little girls. What would you do?

The clothing worn by women in Bangladesh is not a saree as it is in India. It is called a sharee. It is the same thing. It is about 15 yards of cloth. And you know, they drape it over their shoulders and wrap it around them like a skirt. It is very attractive. It is their national dress.

Try to imagine how this man felt as he took each of his daughters and climbed with each of his daughters into the top of a coconut tree. He took each child and their sharee, the 15 yards of cloth, and he tied each child into the top of a coconut tree. He would come back down and get the next one. Perhaps he started with the smallest one. Was she afraid when he had to say "stay here, I'm going to get your sister." One by one this man tied his daughters into the top of a tree with their little dresses. There was no more room in the tree. He took his wife and tied her into the top of another tree. And finally, he lashed himself into the top of a tree with nothing to do but wait for night to fall and the most horrible floods and tidal wave in recent history to attack his family. There was nothing he could do.

Sometimes love means we cannot do anything. Sometimes you have done everything you can do to raise that child and then you have got to send them out in the world on their own, don't you? Sometimes we have done everything we can do in the hospital and your best friend is still dying there. There is nothing else we can do. Sometimes you have done everything you can to save your business or your family, and there is nothing else you can do. That is faith on the cutting edge. That is where faith looks at us and says, "Sometimes love requires that we let go."

I wondered what that man felt when it got so dark he could not see his babies in the tree anymore. I was haunted, wondering what went through his mind when the rains started beating on him, and the winds started making the trees sway back and forth, when he could hear the thunder of a tidal wave rolling right towards him and his family. What did he think about? Will any of them survive? If I die, who will look after his family? When the light comes back on and it is morning, will I look over there and see that all my little girls are dead. Which one could I do without? If the youngest dies, how will I feel? I count on the oldest one. What would happen to me? What if my wife is swept away? And beneath them the flood raged and all around them the storm beat down. That man had no choice. He had to just let go. Sometimes love means you have to just let go.

When the sun came up the next day, all of his family had survived that horrible experience. Look at what the Book says. "Whatever is born of God conquers the world." This is the victory that conquers the world, our faith.

Presbyterians do not use words like victory much. Didn't we even take "Onward Christian Soldiers" out of the hymnal because somebody would be upset at the idea of conquering? But here it is in the Book. The writer is talking about Jesus Christ living in our lives giving us the strength to conquer problems of letting go. He gives us the courage to sit there just take it. If Jesus can die for me, I can live for him. No matter how tough the times are, the word conquer and victory are very common to you. You have heard them more times than you can imagine.

I brought something I want to show you so for the rest of your days you will remember what I am telling you today. The word conquer and victory come from the same Greek word, *nike*. *Nike*, of course, makes sporting shoes of all different types. The word means "Victory".

In Jesus, Christ is your victory. In Jesus Christ, we can overcome the problems of our families, our hearts and the issues of how do I love someone who is unlovable? You do what their slogan is: Just do it! I like that.

I got a telegram from Bangladesh one time. It was Christmas. One of the things we do there is immunize children against polio. That means you give them three shots a couple of weeks apart. You give them a shot, two weeks later you give them another shot and then two weeks later you give them another shot and they will not get polio. We give them these shots just like you get. The vaccine has to be kept cold or it will spoil. The telegram said that five hundred doses of polio vaccine had spoiled. It was no good

We have to have it or 500 children would be exposed to polio. Some would die from that. I got in my car and I went to the drug store and I said to the pharmacist, I need polio vaccine. He said, "Sure." "I really do, 500 doses." He said, "Alright." He got it for me.

Then I went to Kroger, the grocery store, and I bought a great old big butter ball turkey. It was Christmastime. I got some of these blue things that you freeze. I froze the blue things, and I froze the turkey, and I kept the vaccine cold. I took it all out at the same time and I put it in an ice chest.

I check the ice chest as my luggage at the Atlanta airport. I flew from Atlanta to London, from London to Bombay, Bombay to Calcutta, from Calcutta to Dhaka, Bangladesh and then out into the bush and guess what? We got to eat a Butterball turkey for Christmas in Bangladesh, and we got to immunize every child we could find. Sometimes you just have to do things like that.

You look around here at this church family, and while we are all smiles, and we look so pretty on a day like this, inside the hearts of some of us, we are broken.

Inside the minds of some of us, we are carrying a weight that we cannot begin to bear. Some of us have struggles, hopes and yearnings that go beyond what any of the rest of us can understand. Some of us know what we should do, but we don't do it. We have a world of possibilities for Jesus Christ.

As I look at our economy, as I look at health care in the United States, as I look at Haiti, Zambia, Zaire, Bangladesh, the remains of the Soviet Union, the new Europe....the list goes on and on and I see in that long list...the wonderful possibilities for Christians like you and me no longer provides us with the privilege of just sitting there and taking it. It is no longer time for Christians to just let go. This point in history is the time for Christians to clear our minds to just do it!

Consider the question. Who is it that conquers the world? The one who believes that Jesus is the Son of God. Turn that question into an answer. The ones who believe that Jesus Christ is the Son of God are the ones who will change the world.

The Cart before the Horse

John 14:8-14

It meant a lot to me that Buddy would invite me to lunch. Buddy and I had become good friends during a difficult time in his life, and it appeared that Buddy was doing his best to put the pieces back together. Buddy had been a law student at Memphis State University. To help his study habits, he found it would be a little easier if he supplemented his diet with illegal drugs. Well, just like everyone who does illegal drugs, Buddy's law career got set aside for a profession aimed at feeding his growing drug habit. Buddy's specialty became robbing banks. Buddy was arrested, put into the jail in which I served as the chaplain, and we became friends.

After somewhere around six months in jail, Buddy managed to get released on bail. Having posted his bail bond, he was a free man waiting to go to trial. He called me and said he wanted to take me to lunch to thank me for my kindness and encouragement to him while he was incarcerated. He took me to one of the nicest restaurants in Memphis.

At that time, the restaurant was called the Top of the 100. It was one of those restaurants that, in the early 70's, revolved and gave you a chance to eat and see the entire city. Anyone sitting in that restaurant would never have supposed that Buddy and I were any more than two business colleagues or old friends sharing a leisurely lunch. I didn't think anything else about it until a week or so later when there was a knock on my office door in the jail.

Ted Gunderson was the Director of the West Tennessee District of the Federal Bureau of Investigations (FBI). He came into my office, closed the door and greeted me in his usual cheerless manner. He asked me where I had eaten lunch a week before and I asked him what did he want to know? Was he looking for somewhere to go to lunch? He pulled out a small note pad and told me that on such and such day at such and such time, I had eaten lunch at the Top of the 100 restaurant. I agreed and asked why that was important. He went on to read from his little pad that I had eaten lunch with my friend, Buddy. I said that was also true. He then informed me with a grin like a Cheshire cat that Buddy had robbed a bank in the Whitehaven section of Memphis, timed the street lights, picked me up, took me to lunch on stolen bank money and used me as his alibi. I never would have guessed it. I thought I was having lunch with one person when all the while I was having lunch with someone else. I really did not know Buddy after all.

Well you see, this was Philip's problem. Philip had spent years with Jesus. They had traveled together, he had seen the miracles of our Lord, he had shared the words of Jesus, yet he still was not able to understand that Jesus was the Messiah. That is why he asked the question, "Lord, show us the Father and that will be enough for us." This is one of the few times when Jesus is truly exasperated with the disciples. Look at what he says.

"Don't you know me, Philip, even after I have been among you such a long time? Anyone who has seen me has seen the Father. How can you say, 'Show us the Father'? Don't you believe that I am in the Father, and that the Father is in me? The words I say to you are not just my own. Rather, it is the Father, living in me, who is doing his work. Believe me when I say that I am in the Father and the Father is in me; or at least believe on the evidence of the miracles themselves. I tell you the truth, anyone who has faith in me will do what I have been doing. He will do even greater things than these, because I am going to the Father. And I will do whatever you ask in my name, so that the Son may bring glory to the Father. You may ask me for anything in my name, and I will do it." John 14:8-14 (NIV)

Which verses caught your attention just then? Were you hearing this as Jesus correcting Philip? Or perhaps what stood out was "anything you ask, I will do." You know we are so much like Philip, aren't we? We want to know that we have seen the Lord and we want to know that we are in the right place at the right time. All believers in Jesus Christ have a desire to do great things for the Kingdom. We want to know that we walk with our hand in Jesus' hand. We want to know that we are going to do greater things than what Jesus did on earth. We want to back it all up by knowing that whatever in the world we ask, the Lord is going to do for us. I guess you could say, spiritually, we are sort of like the fictional character, Walter Mitty.

At times all of us have a vision of ourselves preaching to the millions or crashing through the jungles of Central America or Africa to carry the gospel to remote tribes. We have these wonderfully challenging visions of actually playing a part in changing the world for Jesus Christ, but if the truth were known, we are really more like Roseanne and Dan. Can you not just see them?

They have been to church for a couple of days, they have gotten excited during revival, they start dreaming dreams and maybe one of those dreams is that Dan wants to be a missionary. They are sitting around the breakfast table talking about it. Dan says, "We are going to sell everything we have and give it to the poor and go to Africa." They look at each other and finally they go, "yeah, right," and they slide back into their bowls of cereal and forget about it.

You know we basically do not do anything really for the Kingdom of God. Every now and then we get a little excited about it and we think maybe great things can happen, but truth be known, in most of our spiritual lives, there is very little to get excited about.

Think back. In the last week how many of us had an exciting answer to prayer? How many of us feel that the Lord has whispered in our ear and given us the assurance of His input and direction? How many of us have seen a miracle? I would like to share with you why it is that I believe we are not doing those greater things for the Kingdom of God. I want to share with you why I believe that most of us just have a ho-hum spiritual life if we have that at all.

If you look at John 14:12 (NASB) Jesus said,

> *"Truly, truly, I say to you, he who believes in Me, the works that I do, he will do also; and greater works than these he will do; because I go to the Father."*

Now my question for you is how many of us are putting the cart before the horse? How can we do the greater things than these Jesus speaks of if we are not doing the basic things? How did Jesus ask Philip to recognize Him? By His words and His works. Jesus said if you believe in Him you will speak the words that He speaks and you will do the things that He does. Jesus further said that you will do greater things than what He did if you believe in Him. I want to tell you about some friends of mine. They have every strike in the world going against them. They are not rich; they are poor. They are not physically attractive; they are physically ugly. They are all handicapped; they are all physically disfigured, and they are all blind.

If we looked at this group by the standards of this world, we would imagine that these people could do very little that would actually make any difference in the life of anybody anywhere in the world. To top it all off, these unfortunate people live in a very remote village in South Korea.

Someone decided that these people were of worth to Jesus Christ and they shared the gospel with them. Out of this, these men who were blind and so desperately disfigured felt a hunger within their souls to learn more about the Word of God. So they began to study Scripture, and they began to memorize the Word. The Word and then the deeds. Now, it took them 25 years to do it, but one group of these men memorized the entire Bible. The other group, not being quite as pious as the first group, was only able to memorize the New Testament, but they did it. Now again, I want to remind you that these men are severely disfigured, they are all blind, they are all old, handicapped, and they all suffer from the long-term effects of leprosy.

Now aside from simply memorizing the Bible, they decided that perhaps there was something they could do for the Kingdom of God and to that end, they came up with a bunch of harmonicas. They formed a harmonica choir and even though they could not see each other, they could hear one another. This choir is magnificent.

They spent their days memorizing Scripture and rehearsing on their harmonicas until their big break came. They were asked to perform in their local church. I am sure they were nervous because they do not get outside very often since many people find them physically unattractive, and for some, that is difficult to handle. With fear and trepidation, the choir performed on their harmonicas and the response was overwhelming. Overnight they became a sensation throughout the church in South Korea.

They traveled all over the country, performing for churches, children, schools, seminaries, conferences and gatherings and, as they performed, they raised a tremendous amount of money. Out of their words came works that they never had imagined to be possible and out of their works came a ministry that to this day brings them great pride and a sense of satisfaction for the Lord.

These leprosy patients, who are so disfigured, who are so blind, who are so helpless and so poor, take all the money they raise and give it to children who they say are worse off than they are. Children who are, in fact, orphans on the streets of Seoul, South Korea. These leprosy patients have gone from the word to the deed and, undoubtedly, have accomplished far greater things than they ever could have dreamed or imagined. These people who had so little were willing to make a difference in the world by giving everything away. Christian, how much more could we, who have so much more, accomplish in the name of Jesus Christ? I believe if we put the Word first, followed by our deeds, we would discover that we too could accomplish greater things than we ever imagined.

The village of Mercery in Haiti is a classic example of a small village controlled by evil. While visiting the village, the voodoo priest would not allow us to come in and drill a well. We also could not hold church services or have school for children or adults. The voodoo priest controlled it all. In spite of his uncompromising control, one woman virtually escaped from the village of Mercery and came to our hospital in Léogâne. She was desperately ill. Several things happened while this woman was a patient in our hospital.

The woman began getting well physically. While she was at the hospital, she renounced voodoo and gave her life to Jesus Christ. The witch doctor in the village heard about these things, came to the hospital, took the woman and claimed he would cure her back in the village. Shortly after the woman returned to the village, she died. The impact of her death was amazing, for the villagers knew that this woman had, in fact, been getting well in our hospital. They knew that this woman had renounced voodoo and had given her life to Jesus Christ. They knew that this woman died at the hands of the voodoo priest, her son. When he could not save his own mother's life, they gathered around him and said, "obviously your power is broken" and that village was set free.

Around the world, the Presbyterian Church is doing amazing things, one village at a time. If you traveled to Zambia, you would see that we have invested over $1 million in our most remote bush hospital in that country. It now has full electricity and 120 beds. The entire facility has been renovated and is now considered one of the best hospitals in Zambia. Former Zambian President Frederick Chiluba visited the hospital when he heard of the great things you have done in that part of the world.

Go to Haiti where the village of Mercery has been set free and to the Presbyterian hospital in Léogâne, which now contains a three-story addition, doubling the amount of bed space we have to offer.

Go to Bangladesh where the slogan for our work is John 10:10b (NKJV), "I have come that they may have life, and that they may have it more abundantly." We have just finished building the Karamtola Clinic north of Dhaka. Fourteen thousand people will receive healthcare because of this church, and many other Presbyterian churches.

Many people wonder, "What can one person do that will make a difference for Jesus Christ?" For many years, Jim Boyce was your medical missionary in Ometepec, Mexico. Jim's career was spent training, caring, sharing, and healing in the name of Christ in a remote hospital in Ometepec. His goal was to teach others so that when he left the hospital it would be under the ministry of competent, educated, Christian Mexican physicians. Several of the young men in his area were literally brought under his wings. He taught them to read, he led them to Christ, and he encouraged them in their education and saw to it that they were able to finish their studies at the university and at medical school. By the time they completed their education and returned to the hospital, it was time for Jim Boyce to come home.

He felt a sense of satisfaction for his accomplishments, but like all of us, he continued to wonder if the impact he made was really going to be a lasting one. He did not know if he had just turned out some good guys who were now physicians or if the hospital would remain a beacon of Christian hope in a desperate situation. It was not until almost 10 years after his retirement that Jim learned of the fruit of his ministry.

The hospital at Ometepec was ravaged by a horrible earthquake. As the walls were shaking and bricks were coming loose, patients, visitors and staff panicked. As they screamed, they ran for the exits and they dove through the windows trying to protect themselves. Jim Boyce learned that as the buildings collapsed the young Christian physicians he had led to Christ and had encouraged with his words and his deeds, literally placed their own bodies over the bodies of patients who could not leave their beds. These physicians were willing to give their lives to protect those individuals in their charge.

Let me remind you that greater things than these you will do! Whatever you ask in Jesus' name, Jesus will answer. Today the call for you and for me is to realize that before we can accomplish the greater challenge that is before us, we must begin to incorporate the Word of God and the compassionate deeds of Christ in our everyday lives. Only then will we be able to ask for things in His name and have it done. We will also be able to do those things that will enable us to complete the mission set before us as a church and as individuals. I am grateful for that spiritual guidance and for the hope that comes along with it and I hope you are thankful as well.

> *Precious Lord, thank you for the reminder that through your blood we are able to do greater things here on earth. May we not limit your presence in our lives? Help us, God, to surrender everything unto you and allow you to empower us to accomplish mighty things in the name of your Son, Jesus Christ. Give to us boldness and courage to step out into the unknown, granting us eyes to see a world as you see it. Grant us to a heart full of compassion that enables us to love as you loved, Jesus. May your mercy and grace rise up within us daily as we minister to a lost and dying world. In Jesus' name I pray, Amen.*

The First Thing I Forget

Matthew 28:16-20 (NASB)

"But the eleven disciples proceeded to Galilee, to the mountain which Jesus had designated. When they saw Him, they worshiped Him; but some were doubtful. And Jesus came up and spoke to them, saying, 'All authority has been given to me in heaven and on earth. Go therefore and make disciples of all the nations, baptizing them in the name of the Father and the Son and the Holy Spirit, teaching them to observe all that I commanded you; and lo, I am with you always, even to the end of the age' "

I love to travel and represent Christ around the world. You meet the most amazing people, so my stories are always true. I do not have to make these up! In one such story, I named the woman, Ms. Mattie Mae Magnolia, a fine Southern woman of Meridian, Mississippi. Now, I met Ms. Mattie Mae Magnolia at Trinity Presbyterian Church in that lovely, little Southern town. Ms. Mattie Mae Magnolia of Meridian, Mississippi, a fine Southern woman, looked at me and said, "I have a story to tell you that is desperately true." I have every reason to believe her.

Ms. Mattie Mae Magnolia told me that she had an opportunity to visit what she referred to as the "Nawthurn" United States. While at a particular social function a group of "nawthurn" gentlemen recognized that Ms. Mattie Mae

Magnolia was in fact from the Bible Belt. One of the "nawthurn" gentlemen spoke to the other and said that he believed beyond a shadow of a doubt that Ms. Mattie Mae Magnolia of Meridian, Mississippi, a fine Southern woman, could in fact name all 12 of the disciples. Well, just as she had learned at the Mississippi State College for Women, Ms. Mattie Mae Magnolia said, "Of course, I can name all 12 of the disciples and she began to recite them. Lee, Jackson, Longstreet, Bragg, Johnson, Beauregard, Van Dorn, Buckner, Polk, Forrest, Morgan, and Taylor." At which time one of the "nawthurn" gentlemen looked at the other and said, "You see, I told you she could name all 12 of the disciples." Now, in case you did not get that, Ms. Mattie Mae Magnolia of Meridian, Mississippi, a fine Southern woman, just spouted off a list of 12 very famous Confederate generals from our recent war of Northern Aggression.

Truth be known, most of us cannot even name the real disciples, 12 of the most important people in history. Think about that. Give it a try. We get the easy ones, which are Matthew, Mark, Luke, and John. Our mind then begins to scramble for other names. Hum, Peter, Paul, and Mary? Amos and Andy? Little Orphan Annie? Barabbas? Barnabas? We get some of them. I mean these are 12 of the most important people in history and most of us cannot name them and truth be known, we know very little about the disciples. The good news is hopefully we know much more about Jesus Christ. Today, what I want to do is take the remaining 11 disciples. I want to take one missionary and I want to take us and put it all in a pile and stir it up and see what we can learn from a very familiar passage of

Scripture. Perhaps we will observe some things we have never noticed before. Now let's begin with a question, "Where are the disciples in this text?" The disciples are on a mountain. Now which mountain are they upon? Mount Nebo, Mount Ararat? Which mountain are they on? Ah! The mountain to which Jesus had directed them. So the disciples are where the Lord wanted them to be. What are they doing? They saw the Lord and they worshiped Him. They are doing what God wanted them to do. So the disciples are where God wants them and they are doing what the Lord wants them to do, but some doubted.

Doubt is nothing more than the Lord whispering in your ear and saying, "Maybe there is more." Bill Washburn is the missionary we'll discuss. He works in the former Zaire. He works in the center of the country and his job is to be an evangelist. Bill travels village to village, pillar to post, sharing the Good News of Jesus Christ and equipping the church to do the same. When we find Bill, he is on the side of a road, his truck is broken down, he has a flat tire, and since I am much younger, I am the one changing the tire while Bill tells me the story of his life.

Bill had been on the road for two weeks. He was tired. He was coming home. He said he felt like a horse heading to the barn when he came around a curve in the jungle path and there it was! For us, it's a wreck on the interstate or it's a traffic jam. Maybe it's construction, but for Bill a tree had fallen across the road. Bill was traveling with a companion. They had no chain saw, they had no chains, and they realized they couldn't get the tree out of the road and they were stuck. That meant they had to turn around, work their way through the jungle and they would end up spending the night. They had to try to find a way to get back to Bill's base at Bulape. Without thinking about the question, "am I where God wants me and am I doing what the Lord wants me to do," we leave Bill as he turns his truck around and heads off into the African sunset.

Okay, we know where the disciples are, we know where Bill is, what about you? Are you where God wants you in life and are you doing what the Lord wants you to do with your life? If we could get alone, get quiet, go sit by a campfire, walk on quail trails, fish in a pond, I think you might sit with me and say, "You know Ben, most of the time life is okay. I get up, I go to work, I look after the kids, I clean the house, and I cook the meals. I go to meetings, I go to church, and I try to love my family. I guess pretty much I could say yes I suppose I am where God wants me and for the most part I am doing what He wants me to do. But you know, Ben, there are times, when I think I just cannot get up and do it one more day. There are times when I think that there must be something more that God wants me to do with my life. That's when all of those doubts come creeping in on me."

Again, remember doubt is nothing more than the Lord giving you a little nudge and saying maybe there is more out there. Maybe you need to explore what else you can do to serve in God's Kingdom. Bill had to turn the truck around and he had to head back through the jungle. You really don't do much talking in times like that. The truck is so loud and you are pounding through the bush. It is hot in those trucks and the air conditioner is the first thing that goes, so the hours drag by and you do not say a word to each other. It gets dark, you turn on the headlights in the forest, and again, you hear the gears grinding, you are bumping up and down. You really wear the seatbelt pretty tight so that it more or less holds you against the seat and you are not just beat to pieces.

Bill said they were driving along through the jungle, and they came around another curve and the headlights shined on somebody standing in the middle of the jungle path. It was the tallest woman Bill Washburn had ever seen in Africa. Her arms were held out straight from her side as if she was forming a cross. She was wearing a white hooded robe that went all the way to the ground and every bit of exposed skin was painted white. Rather than run over the woman, Bill stopped the truck right there in a part of the forest he had never been in before. Before he could say a word to his traveling companion, they were surrounded by people who were wearing long white robes and were painted white. They pulled Bill out of one side of the truck and they pulled his buddy out the other side. They pushed them off into the jungle as they were being led toward the sounds of drums pounding. They could smell torches that were burning while they were shoved into the middle of a clearing where there was one tall stake that went straight up in the air. You talk about having doubt in your life!

I looked at Bill and said, "Bill, what did you do?" Well he looked at me like I was crazy and he said, "Well, Ben, I prayed. I prayed." If I had prayed at all in that situation, I probably would have prayed, "Oh Lord, I hope my buddy makes it back to the truck because I'm out of here!" But, you see since Bill Washburn was where God wanted him to be. He was doing what the Lord wanted him to do even in a time of doubt, because of that obedience, Bill could claim the next verse of Scripture. Jesus said, "All authority on heaven and on earth has been given to me." If we are where God wants us to be, and if we are doing what the Lord wants us to do, then that same power and that same authority is ours as well. As soon as I get a temptation, as soon as I get discouraged, as soon as life goes bad, that is the first thing I forget. It is so easy for me to forget that the power and the authority of Jesus Christ is mine in my life, not because of me, but because of Jesus Christ.

Oh, Bill, what happened to Bill? The drums are pounding, the torches are burning, everybody is in their dress whites, and the drums stop. The great big tall woman who had been standing in the middle of the road walked up to Bill Washburn, looked him in the eye, and said, "We knew that you were coming tonight." Bill looked at her and said, "You could not know I was coming tonight. I am lost. I am trying to work my way back to Bulape. I have never been in this part of the forest before. You've got the wrong man." That woman looked Bill in the eye and said, "We knew you were coming tonight. We serve the unknown god and he told us that you were coming tonight to tell us his name. Who is the unknown god?"

Because Bill Washburn was simply where God wanted him to be, simply doing what the Lord wanted him to do even in the midst of great doubt and fear, because of those very simple things, Bill Washburn was given the incredible privilege of telling an entire tribe about all the things that Jesus taught him. He was also able to make disciples of that entire village of people, was able to baptize them in the name of the Father, the Son, and the Holy Spirit and began teaching them to obey everything that Jesus commanded. Wow! If that does not give you goose bumps, something is wrong.

We know where the disciples were. They were on the mountain. We know where Bill Washburn was. He was fulfilling his call, serving in the center of Africa. The question for you has got to be, are you where God wants you and are you doing what the Lord wants you to do, or do you need to make some changes? Do you need to stop an addiction that is killing you? Do you need to pick up an old dream the Lord gave you? Are there some habits, attitudes, and selfish perspectives that you need to put aside? Is Jesus prompting you to write that check to support your church, a missionary or a ministry? Are there some areas of unforgiveness that you simply need to get over because the offense was so very long ago?

Is it time for you to move closer to the Lord so that perhaps you could begin remembering the power and authority Christ has in your life? I challenge you to take a few minutes today to examine your life. If you need to make some changes, I want you to do that in the sure and certain knowledge of the words of our Lord when He said, "I am with you always to the very end of the age." To that I am grateful and I hope you are too. God bless you. Stay strong and God bless America!

> *Gracious, Lord, thank you for the opportunities*
> *you give to me and for the divine appointments you*

provide me in order to lead others to the saving knowledge of you. Forgive me, Lord, for those times when I feel you're leading and I hesitate and fail to move forward in obedience. Forgive me too for those instances when I have allowed fear and doubt to dictate the path I would choose instead of trusting your leading and guiding hand in my life. Increase my faith and trust in you, I pray and give to me a more willing spirit and obedient heart to follow after you, no matter what. In Jesus' precious name I pray, Amen.

The Formula for Life

Keep alert, stand firm in your faith, be courageous, be strong, and let everything you do be done in love.

One more time:

Keep alert, stand firm in your faith, be courageous, be strong, and let everything you do be done in love.

As I matured, I have discovered that I have picked up a few habits along the way that I just need to get rid of, and I want you to know that I am getting rid of one of those habits, right here, right now, this morning. I am going to stop it. I am not going to do it anymore. It isn't going to happen ever again. I am finished, I am done. DUN! I want you to humor me on this. On three I want you to stand up and sit back down again and I will show you what I mean. Ready, 1-2-3, sit back down again. Now, how many of you either did this or heard someone do this when they go up…Hmmmm. You know what that is? I have decided that this is my brain arguing with my body. That's my brain saying "get up" and my body saying "no, I don't want to do that, it's gonna hurt." My brain says "I don't care, get up anyway." So I am going to get up, but I am going to grunt when I do it.

I have learned that if I don't grunt, it doesn't hurt. No grunt…no pain. Say that with me. No grunt…no pain. One more. No grunt…no pain. Now today when you leave church and you get in the car, I don't want to hear a grunt in that parking lot….and that's today's tidbit for living.

Now I'm a big believer that one thought leads to another, that leads to another, and you tell me if this isn't true. When I was talking about your brain arguing with your body, one thought lead to another and you were thinking about the apostle Paul and the church at Corinth, weren't you? Huh, huh, see I knew that. Did I tell ya? What can I say? I knew that was going to happen.

The church at Corinth is just like a whole lot of us who argue between their brains and their body. The church at Corinth argued about everything! What you can eat and cannot eat, what you can drink and cannot drink, who Jesus was and who Jesus wasn't, and into the middle of that the apostle Paul had to stop everything he was doing and try to get them back on track by allowing the Lord to speak through him and he wrote the letters we call 1st and 2nd Corinthians.

Paul is like a football coach. I don't know about you, but when I played football back "in the day," we'd go into the locker room at halftime and no matter how we were doing the football coach would pace back and forth and read you the riot act and just let us have it and then it was like the lights went on and he would think, "I'm beating them up and they have to go back out there and play so I better inspire them." So then he would find something exciting to say. Paul did the same thing. He beat up the church at Corinth and then said "OK, keep alert. Stand firm in your faith. Be courageous, be strong, and let everything you do be done in love. Now get out there and play the game."

The muse is upon me. I have a poem.

I was shocked, confused, bewildered as I entered Heaven's door.

Not by the beauty of it all or the lights or its décor,

it was the folks in Heaven who made me sputter and gasp.

The thieves, the liars, the sinners, the alcoholics, and the trash.

There stood the kid from seventh grade who swiped my lunch money twice!

Next to him was my old neighbor who never said anything nice!

And Bob, who I always thought was rotting away in hell,

was sitting pretty on Cloud Nine, looking incredibly well.

I nudged Jesus, "Hey what's the deal? I'd love to hear your take.

How did all these sinners get up here? God must have made a mistake.

Why is everyone so quiet, so somber? Give me a clue."

"Hush child", Jesus said, "they're all in shock. No one thought they'd be seeing you."

How many of you believe in Jesus as your Lord and Savior? Raise your right hand for me. Then let me ask you something. Why is it that if you believe in Jesus as your Lord and Savior, so many of you leave him right here when you leave the church? Oh, after a good Sunday you might go say grace over lunch, you may say it Sunday night even, but then throughout the rest of the week it's all you, isn't it? You did that. I did this. Hey mom, I did this. When Paul says "keep alert," he is actually saying, "Christian, Christian, Jesus died on the cross and rose again from the dead specifically so that you could keep alert to the presence of God in your life".

Christian you do not go through life by luck and coincidence. Every step you take, every time you take a breath, you are held in the palm of God's hand and everything you experience and realize in your life is held in His hand and everything's gonna be all right if you simply keep alert for God's presence in your life.

My friend, Allison, had a very sick daddy in the hospital. Her dad did not know the Lord. Allison sat beside his hospital bed and explained to him, "Daddy, you do not have much longer. I have to get going. I want you to know something. This chair is going to stay here, and I want you to imagine the Lord sitting in this chair and you need to have a talk with Him before you go." She walked out and he died during the night, but when they found Allison's daddy, his hand was in that chair. That touched that woman's life so deeply that she sent you something today.

Right out the door in the Narthex on the right there is a little table. These are on that table. There are also ROW caps and mugs, please take all of that with you. Please take it. Especially take one of these. If you open this box, there is nothing more than a little chair. See sometimes we need concrete reminders of God's invisible grace. We need to be able to touch something, to taste it, to feel it, and that is what this is. She wants you to take this chair and set it on your desk at work, put it in the car, give it to a friend, set it beside the bed to remind yourself to keep alert to the presence of God in your life. Because if you do, the amazing thing is that this will help you clarify the very things that you believe and you will stand firm for your faith.

I was embedded with a combat striker team in the eastern Behala Province of Iraq and you prayed over me before I went. There are some incredible people in Iraq that you would never meet. One is a Christian Iraqi who kept alert for God's presence in his life and it has enabled him to stand firm in what he believes God wants him to do; and, believe it or not, this man has spent his life building Christian radio stations across Iraq. Think about that.

Saddam was not pleased with that. Saddam put this man on the list of people who needed to be exterminated for the greater good. Well, apparently one of our first cruise missiles came through the very window of the very office that held all the records of the people that Saddam wanted to exterminate, and they were all blown up and to this day that incredible man is now working his way across northern Iraq building Christian radio stations to share the gospel with the Kurdish people in the north.

If you keep alert for God's presence in your life, you will stand firm in your faith. And when you stand firm in your faith, it's going to give you a tremendous sense of courage. A striker is like a mechanized vehicle that carries 12 of our young soldiers. I had fired one of my staff, I told him to go join the army and grow up. He did and he became a lieutenant and he commands four of these striker units.

I embedded with his platoon of soldiers. That means because I do Christian radio I went there to broadcast the gospel from Iraq, to preach to the soldiers, to pray with them, but when you go as a journalist, you can do anything the troops can do. That means I'm in combat with them, I'm at their base with them, I sleep where they sleep, I eat where they eat, and I go everywhere they go and one of the things we did was get the word that the bad guys are down the road, five kilometers to the right. We piled in the strikers and everyone was good to go, zoomed down the road, and you watch these incredible, young Americans as they deploy into the forest and go through the woods picking a fight with the bad guys. It is just incredible!

One of my jobs was to try to get around in front of the platoon so I could catch these young men as they were in a combat mission coming through the forest and film this. You are so engrossed in doing this. You are in your bullet-proof gear, you have your helmet on, and you are sitting there filming this as this intense moment happens and I felt a hand on my shoulder. I thought oh my goodness, that's it, I'm just gone forever.

I turned around and standing behind me is Sergeant Jeffrey Shipp. He is the platoon sergeant for this platoon of soldiers. He is the "old man." Sergeant Shipp is probably pushing 33-34 years old! He is tattooed from head to toe. He is very creepy looking. I've gotta give you that. In the south we would describe him as having a lot of "rough edges." His men love him because he knows how to look after them and he knows how to bring them back alive!

Sergeant Shipp knelt beside me and very quietly put his head up to mine and spoke into my ear and said, "You know, there are snipers out here. There are landmines, booby traps, and trip wires. How about this? How about you letting me go first and we will be okay." I turned around and watched that young American march off into combat and I thought, "Lord, that's the personification of courage." It comes from two French words Cour which means heart and Age which means old. Courage is an old heart. It's a heart that knows you can break it pretty easy, but it's hard to kill a heart.

It's a heart that has been strengthened by knowing God's presence is in your life. I did sit at the base later on and Sergeant Shipp and I had a chance to visit and he is very much alert to God's presence in his life. He knows exactly what he believes, and he stands firm in that and because of that, Sergeant Shipp has the courage to lead his men into battle. I want you to know he brought them all home safe and sound.

Keep alert for God's presence in your life, stand firm in your faith, you will have a great sense of courage, and it's underwritten with strength. And it's not like physical strength that waxes and wanes, you know that. It's a spiritual strength that is hard to describe except for Haitians.

When Haiti collapsed, all the rats came out.... the literal rats and the figurative rats...came out of all the rubble of Haiti. My friend, Pastor Louie, has a successful ministry out of Port-au-Prince, outside of the capital city.

A successful ministry is a little church and a little school surrounded by a wall where a dedicated pastor does evangelism and education, trying to raise some strong, young Christian people in Haiti. His wife, Jackie, is very much a part of this and when all the rats came out Jackie fell prey to the new trend in developing nations.

Jackie got kidnapped in the midst of all this horror. Pastor Louie responded just like he would. He is absolutely at the end of his rope. His faith is being tested and pulled and stretched, and three days into this ordeal, the phone rings and it's his wife, Jackie. She has found a cell phone. "Oh thank you Jesus. Jackie, where are you and we will come and get you?" She said, "No not yet, I'll call you back." And, she hangs up on him. Gentleman, what would you do? Second question, are you married to a Jackie? If you are, don't say anything now, we don't want to start a problem. This goes on for a week. She calls him three or four different times and each time hangs up on the dear man. Finally, she said, "I think this is where I am, come and get me." Pastor Louie gets the cops, they break in the door, in they come, and there stands his wife Jackie and in front of her on their knees are her three kidnappers begging forgiveness and have given their lives to Jesus. That's strength. That is strength.

Do everything you do in love. It's agape, It's that unconditional, unselfish love of God, and Jesus that takes hands like this and opens them up to the whole wide world. It is that love that stopped my young men in Vietnam.

We worked from Quay and Da Nang and southwest. If you were there it's the same rice patties. If you were there it's the same dykes. If you were there, it's the same trails.

Drew and his men are west of Da Nang and they are coming through the rice patties. They come around a turn, and they stop because they find a woman and a little boy sitting on top of a pile of bricks. Next to the bricks is their home. It is made out of cardboard and discarded tin. It's a little dog kennel. They ask what her story is.

The father and the older son had died. That's all they were told. This woman had nothing in the world, except hope. And whenever she got a few pennies, or whenever she found one, walking to town or in town, she would either buy or pick up a discarded brick and bring it back to her hovel and put that brick in the pile believing that one day she would have enough bricks to build a home.

What is the love of Jesus? It's the stuff that made those young men stop right there on the spot and they laid the foundation for that woman's home. They dug around in their pockets and found the little bit of money they had, and they found a man who said he would build a house for her. So they gave that man the money and trusted him and they went on about their way, but the real love of Jesus happened a year later when they had forgotten all about this.

They were walking down that same trail inadvertently heading from one small village to the next and they came upon that woman and her home. It has two concrete columns out front. It has a cement roof. It will stand up under the storms of Vietnam and it has an incredibly overwhelming young mother and her child who live there.

She came out and made eye contact with my staff member. They had no idea they would run into each other ever again and right there on that trail. Oh, imagine the joy! She threw her arms around my men and they all stood there weeping and crying. Christian, that's the love of God in Jesus! When something impossible rises out of a rice patty in Vietnam!

It's like a formula, it's a simple formula. You want to know how to live your life? Recognize that Jesus Christ died on the cross and rose again so that you can keep alert to God's presence in your life. That you can stand firm for your faith. That you can have a great sense of courage! That you can have strength! That you can live your life in the love of God and Jesus Christ!

Do you remember that stuff about how one thought leads to another? Do you remember that? Let me ask you something. When I just said what I said, you tell me this isn't true. One thought led to another and as I was reading that verse to you again, in your mind, your next thought was about King Leonidas and the Greeks, wasn't it? Go ahead and shake your head. See, I knew that!!

You remember Leonidas; he has 500 guys that are called Spartans. They are soldiers. They have to protect Greece at a place called Thermopylae. They gather and here comes the enemy and the enemy happens to be thousands of Persian soldiers. These fellows are battle hardened, and they are in a bad mood, and they are coming to whip the Greeks. The thousands of these men look down at their 500 little Spartans standing there and think we came all the way here for this? The commander of the Persian army looks at this little gathering of Greek soldiers and he says something very gallant. "Lay down your weapons." King Leonidas gives the greatest answer of all time. In Greek it is *Molon Labe*. It is translated two ways. I'll say the word and then give you the translation. Lay down your weapons, translation number one, "Come and get them" …. that's pretty good. Lay down your weapons, translation number two (and I like this better), "Bring it on." They stood their ground and they whooped the Persian army.

Christian, I don't know if you know this or not? You get about 200 yards beyond the door of this church and you are in a world that looks at Christians and wants to yell at you "Lay down your arms". The church is not significant anymore. Lay down your arms! We are going to sit and fight about the dumbest things while the world goes to the devil. Lay down your arms! I can distract you from the church. I can tempt you away from this. I can help drive your bank account. I can take you away from being involved in this. These are not really your friends. Lay down your arms and give up!

I would say to you that, as Christians, part of the struggle we have is that we understand God's invisible grace, but there are times when we need to be reminded. We need to touch, taste, and feel the presence of God in our lives. That is exactly why we have the sacraments today.

There is a great phrase that we use in the prayer book "for all those who wish to covenant afresh your relationship with Jesus." If you examine your life and you have come into this place afraid, worried about our country, our economy, how many wars is it now, what's the direction our government is going, what's happening in my own community? If you come in here and you have been just thinking about you and not looking for the presence of God in your life, if you have come in here and you would like to pick it up, put it down, take a step, get over it, this is the place to do it. Right here and right now! I call you in the name of the risen Lord, as a believer in Jesus Christ, to come to His table. Covenant afresh your relationship with him so that as you leave here today, you will have decided to keep alert to God's presence in your life. You will have decided to stand firm in your faith. You will have decided to be courageous and strong. You will have decided to do all that you do in the love and for the sake of Jesus who died on the cross for you. I invite you to the Lord's Table. I bless you and you stay strong. God bless America!

The Joyful Accomplishment of Faith

> *"Therefore, brethren, since we have confidence to enter the sanctuary by the blood of Jesus, by the new and living way which he opened for us through the curtain, that is, through his flesh, and since we have a great priest over the house of God, let us draw near with a true heart in full assurance of faith, with our hearts sprinkled clean from evil conscience and our bodies washed with pure water. Let us hold fast the confession of our hope without wavering, for he who promised is faithful; and let us consider how to stir up one another to love and good works, not neglecting to meet together, as is habit of some, but encouraging one another, and all the more as you see the Day drawing near."*
> Hebrews 10:19-25 (RSV)

As I begin this chapter, I am going to draw from some help offered to me by a particular statistician. This friend of mine works in a large office setting, and seems to understand a malady that has affected me severely. Basically, I am tired. Now I have tried to figure out why I am so tired, and I think I have come to my conclusion. I am tired because I am overworked. Do you realize that the population of this country is well over 200 million? An estimated 84 million people are retired. That leaves 116 million people to do the work. There are 75 million in school, which leaves 41 million people to do the work. Of this total, there are 22 million people employed by the government. That leaves 19 million to do the work. An estimated 4 million are in the armed forces, which leaves 15 million to do the work. Take from that total the 14,800,000 people who work for state and city government, and that leaves 200,000 people to do the work. There are 188,000 people in hospitals, so that leaves 12,000 people to do the work. You and me. You are sitting here reading this. No wonder I am tired!

I am so tired that I recently called a friend of mine and asked him for the upcoming Sunday off. I explained to him my dilemma, and he responded with the following, "Before you ask for the day off, consider the following statistics: there are 365 days in the year, you sleep eight hours a day, making 122 days, which subtracted from 365 makes 243 days. You also have eight hours' recreation every day, making another 122 days and that leaves a balance of 121 days. There are 52 Sundays that you do not work at all, which leaves 69 days. You get Saturday afternoon off, this gives 52 half days, or 26 more days that you do not work. This leaves a balance of 43 days. You get an hour off for lunch, which then totals 16 days, leaving 27 days of the year. You get at least 21 days leave every year, so that leaves six days. You get five legal holidays during the year, which leaves only one day to get the job done, and you cannot have that day off!"

I am sure you can see where I am headed with this chapter. I want to talk to you about excuses. Now I do not mean excuses about how to get out of work—we seem to have that pretty well covered. I am not talking to you about excuses for a poor family life. Our society teaches us to do that, and to do that very well!

No, I want to talk to you about why you no longer have an excuse to be an ineffective Christian. You know, someone who claims the name, but never plays the game. In my consideration of this topic, I considered two approaches.

I thought I could make you feel guilty. Preachers are pretty well equipped to make people feel absolutely horrible about the life they live. However, if you already feel guilty, you would feel even worse and probably close the book. If you felt good about yourself, you would realize that this chapter was not directed at you and then you would feel no need to continue reading. Therefore, guilt is out of the question!

I thought that, perhaps, I could scare you with this topic. However, we are Americans. We believe beyond a shadow of a doubt that we will always have another day. We are Americans. What in the world could go wrong? Therefore, it is very difficult to scare Americans into anything substantial.

No, let us be honest. I believe that the Church is ineffective and that most Christians have a very weak spiritual life because of two reasons.

1. Most Christians are tragically ignorant concerning the needs of the world and the Word of God.

2. Most Christians do not want to look like one of "them." You know who "they" are. "They" are the ones who trap you at the office water fountain, and either want to sell you some cleansing product, or tell you about their relationship with Jesus. Most of us find this very intimidating and are

uncomfortable with a discussion about something as wonderful as our own Lord. We do not want to appear like one of "them." Therefore, we hide our Christ-likeness along with some of our other best-kept family secrets. You know the one I am talking about. You really do not want anyone to know about Aunt Lulabelle, who was put in the institution in South Georgia because she was not quite all there! Besides, if our pastor found out how seriously we took our relationship with Christ, he or she might expect something from us! Can you imagine what that would mean? Our pastor might call us to do something. We might just be required to spend some time, effort, or money to serve in the Church! That could cost us our reputation, and even go so far as costing us our lifestyles!

I have actually spoken at session meetings where the pastor introduced me by saying, "This is Ben Mathes. What he has to say won't take very long, and it won't cost us any money, so listen up."

That is silly! I could not remind my colleague on the spot, but unfortunately, he had forgotten something very basic. It is going to cost a great deal of money to change the world for Christ. It is going to take a great deal of effort, and it is going to take a great deal of time. I recall how many times I have heard my boss say to me, "I know this is a difficult task. I know that we will be working late into the night to accomplish this, but guess what, that is our job! That is what we are here to do! Let us get at it!" Christians, believe it or not, changing the world for Jesus Christ is our job. It is not going to be easy, but let us get at it!

Am I Ever Going to Get Out of Here?

I know what some of you are thinking. You believe that I am talking about everyone else—but you. In your own eyes, you are unworthy, you are unlovable, and you are too:

Fat,

Thin,

Young,

Old,

Smart,

Dumb,

Rich,

Poor.

Let us do something different during this chapter. Let us quit thinking about you. Yes, that is right. Take your eyes off of yourself, look towards the ceiling in the room in which you are sitting, and spend time thinking about someone else. Let me tell you who to think about. Think about a person in your life who you consider to be a spiritual heavy weight. Who is the person you know who personifies active, and effective Christianity? Think about that person.

Let me share something with you. That person sings from a hymnal very much like the one you use in your church. That person prays prayers very similar to the ones that you pray. That person reads the same Bible that you may or may not read. In a recent survey, it was tragically discovered that less than 25 percent of Christians read the Bible more than once a month outside of church. This person you're thinking about reads his or her Bible.

What is the biggest difference? I believe that the saint you have described has given God some time. The saint has given God some time to allow His Word to bounce around in the soul of the saint. The saint has spent time meditating, thinking about the Word of God, and has been spiritually nourished by it, just as surely as a starving child is revived by food.

The task before us is at times overwhelming. The suffering of this world and the opportunity to defeat it are great. This holy mission of faith can only be accomplished by Christians who feed upon, who claim, and who incorporate the Word of God into the very fiber of their being. You are called to a destiny. You are called to a higher purpose in life. You are called to look the enemies of our Lord directly in their eyes and stand your ground, empowered by the truth of the gospel.

That is why we chose the Book of Hebrews as our text for this chapter. The writer of the Book of Hebrews was accomplishing several tasks with his text. He was attempting to show a comparison between Christianity and Judaism, Christianity and everything else. In addition, he was offering Christians throughout the ages a handbook for survival. While we did not quote it in our specific text, the writer of the Book of Hebrews defines the gospel in chapter 10 verse 12, "But when Christ had offered for all time a single sacrifice for sins, He sat down at the right hand of God." That is the gospel! Jesus Christ offered a single sacrifice for your sins, died, was resurrected, and is now seated at the right hand of God the Father Almighty!

Therefore, we may now have confidence (faith) to stand before God the Father. Standing in the presence of the Father, we will with all courage find an overwhelming presence of acceptance, reconciliation, forgiveness, and love. We have become God's forgiven army of believers.

While we will find this forgiveness and acceptance, we will also find that we are NOT called to be God's forgiven army standing in dress parade, but without ever firing a shot! Just as surely as we are to receive forgiveness, we are to receive our marching orders as well!

Standing unashamedly and with confidence in the presence of God is what Barclay refers to as the joyful accomplishment of faith. Paul said it a little differently,

> *"For I am sure that neither death, nor life, nor angels, nor principalities, nor things present, not things to come, nor powers, nor height, nor depth, nor anything else in all creation, will be able to separate us form the love of God and Christ Jesus, our Lord."* Romans 8:38-39

Do you feel the power in those words? Read them again. Paul is talking with great conviction and confidence.

As the writer of Hebrews continues, we recognize that because of this confidence we can draw near to the Lord with full assurance of faith. The Latin phrase is wonderful! In Latin, this text says that we can draw near to God with plenty of faith! We are called to hold fast to the confessions of the Church. We are called to hang onto what we believe, for He who promised is faithful!

What have we learned so far? We have learned that because Christ paid the price for our sins, we can stand boldly before our Creator and find acceptance, forgiveness, and a mission! We can cling to the Church and her beliefs, for Christ has promised it and He is faithful. While the words of Paul give us power, the words from the Book of Hebrews give us strength! If Christ is for us, then who can ever be against us?!

Oh, the freedom we experience when we realize the truth of God's Word! For Martin Luther, it gave him the courage to begin the Protestant reformation. David Livingston received the vision to conquer Africa for Jesus Christ. For thousands of missionaries around the world, the Word of God has given them the power to answer a call to serve and live in the most remote parts of the world, and rest in the hope that through the Church the Lord will supply their every need.

For our lives, the Word of God transforms us into active, useful believers in Jesus Christ. We do not have to be tired anymore! We do not have to be defeated anymore! We do not have to be depressed anymore! Instead, "Let us consider how to stir up one another to love and good works, not neglecting to meet together, as is the habit of some, but encouraging one another all the more as you see the Day drawing near." Hebrews 10:24-25

It is agape love that is described in these verses. This is unconditional and unselfish love of God and Jesus Christ that transforms hearts, minds, and wallets that are closed to the needs of the world.

Good works is not simply confined to small acts of charity or kindness. The verse says, "Let us consider…" The Latin word is *considerare*. *Considerare* literally means "to observe the stars." The writer of the Book of Hebrews is telling believers in Jesus Christ that we have the right to set our sights high! Because of the price paid by Jesus Christ, we have the right to dream dreams, see visions, and actually believe that we can play a part in changing the world for Jesus Christ.

Carroll Kakac reminds us that it is all a matter of attitude. "We will know our attitude is on the right track when we are like the small businessman whose clothing store was threatened with extinction. A national chain store had moved in and acquired all the properties on his block. This one particular businessman refused to sell. 'All right then, we will build all around you and put you out of business,' the new competitor said. The day came when the small merchant found himself hemmed in with a new department store stretching out on both sides of his little retail shop. The competitor's banners announced 'Grand Opening!' The merchant countered with a banner stretching across the entire width of his store. It read, 'Main Entrance.'"

Sin is big business in this world. In its most subtle and most blatant forms, the struggles of life have come and announced that they are going to put the Church out of business. I charge you today, dear readers, to take the Word of God to heart. Because Jesus Christ paid the price for our sins, we can have the courage and confidence to place a banner above our hearts that announces Jesus Christ, the main entrance to the way, the truth and the life lived abundantly.

> *Thank you, Jesus, for your sacrifice on the cross. It is through your sacrifice that we have been forgiven of our sins, we have been restored and renewed, and we have been equipped with the power of the Holy Spirit to go forth and serve you in this lost and dying world. Help us to realize your power within us and stir up within us that boldness, assurance and confidence to witness and serve others for you. Help us, too, to encourage one another to hold fast to the mighty faith we have through you, dear Lord. May we walk out this faith daily, bringing you honor and glory in all that we do. Thank you for the wonderful privilege we have in serving you and your people. For I ask these things in your holy, powerful name, Jesus. Amen.*

The Unknown God

Now the eleven disciples went to Galilee to the mountain to which Jesus had directed them. When they saw Him they worshipped Him; but some doubted. And Jesus came and said to them, "All authority in heaven and on earth has been given to me. Go therefore and make disciples of all nations, baptizing them in the name of the Father and of the Son and of the Holy Spirit, teaching them to observe all that I have commanded you; and lo, I am with you always, to the close of the age." Matthew 28: 16-20 (RSV)

Basically, I travel the Church speaking on behalf of Presbyterian medical missions. At times, I feel like a television wrestler. You know, Monday in Atlanta, Tuesday in Jackson, Mississippi, Wednesday in Talladega, Alabama, Thursday in Memphis, Tennessee, etc., etc.! At other times, I feel like the Willard Scott of the Presbyterian Church! No matter where I am, I consistently find that the Church treats me with great love and respect. It is a delightful experience to get to know the Church around the world.

Getting to know the Church means getting to know her members. That in itself is quite an experience! The following story is true. I have changed her name, but she is a member of the Trinity Presbyterian Church, in Meridian, Mississippi. For the sake of illustration, I have named her Miss Mattie Mae Magnolia of Meridian, Mississippi, a fine Southern woman. Now Miss Mattie Mae Magnolia of

Meridian, Mississippi, had an opportunity to visit what some of us refer to as the "Nawthurn United States," while attending a particular social function, Miss Mattie Mae Magnolia of Meridian, Mississippi, a fine Southern woman, was noticed by several of the gentlemen as being a resident of the Bible Belt. Upon realizing this, one of the "Nawthurn" gentlemen remarked that he believed that Miss Mattie Mae Magnolia could in fact name all twelve of the disciples. Without batting an eye and just as she had learned at the Mississippi State College for Women, Miss Mattie Mae Magnolia said, "Of course I can," and she began, "Lee, Jackson, Longstreet, Bragg, Johnston, Beauregard, Van Dorn, Buckner, Polk, Forrest, Morgan, Taylor."

At this point one of the "Nawthurn" gentlemen remarked to the other, "You see, Sir, I told you she could name all twelve of the disciples." And Miss Mattie Mae Magnolia of Meridian, Mississippi, a fine Southern woman retired to her hotel room to further contemplate the mysteries of the Generals of the Confederacy.

Now that raises a good question. I wonder how many of you can name all twelve of the Disciples. Oh, we all remember Peter. I doubt anyone forgets Thomas. Judas was the bad guy. But what about after that? I am amazed at some of the names of the first twelve disciples. Often, I hear names like Paul, Barnabus, Timothy, and Luke mentioned as some of the first twelve disciples! It is absolutely amazing! When we study scripture, I stay further amazed when we are told so very little about these men. These are twelve of the most important men in recorded history, and we know so very little about them. Thank goodness we know so very much about Jesus Christ!

In spite of the paucity of information concerning the disciples, I would still like to use them as models for effective Christian discipleship. In the Matthew 28 text, the remaining eleven disciples represent men following very basic and simple principles that enabled the Lord to use them to bring about change in the world. I realize that this is a very familiar passage of scripture. Many of us have memorized it at one point or another in our lives. However, I also believe that is the exciting part of the text. To study a very familiar passage is to find new insights for living.

I would like to take the remaining eleven disciples, one missionary and ourselves; put them all together and see what we can learn about effective Christian living.

Here is a Bible study tip. As you read scripture, ask yourself some basic questions – who, what, when, and where. Those simple interrogatives will bring scripture to life. Let us look at the first verse. Where are the disciples in this verse? In Galilee! Correct! Where in Galilee? On a mountain! Correct again! Now, let us be more specific. Which mountain are they upon? The one to which the Lord had directed them! Correct, again! Our first basic principle leaps out to greet us! The disciples are where the Lord wants them!

They see the Lord, and what do they do? They worship Him! That is also correct. The disciples are where God wants them and they are doing what the Lord wants them to do.

Tomorrow, you will go through your daily routine. Some of you will go to an office. Others will get your family ready for school and work. Some will call on clients. Others will check on elderly friends. Regardless, we all have a daily routine. There was certain security in the sameness. Bill Washburn is your missionary. He does not go to an office. Instead, he gets in his Toyota Land Cruiser and travels village-to-village, church-to-church in Zaire. Bill is an evangelist. His ministry is to equip the church to do the work of Jesus Christ in the forest of Zaire.

On one particular occasion Bill had been on the road for two weeks. If you travel like I do, two weeks away from home is a long time. It is late in the afternoon. Darkness is about to cover the forest. Bill comes around a curve in the road and it happens. In Atlanta, we call it construction, or a traffic jam. The equivalent in the Forest of Zaire is that someone has knocked a tree across the road. Without thinking, "Am I where God wants me?" "Am I doing what the Lord wants me to do?" Bill stops his jeep.

There is a man sitting on top of the tree. He tells Bill that the tree has been knocked across the road on purpose. The bridge has been washed out. The tree was knocked across the road to keep people from driving into the river. In order to get home to Kananga, Bill must follow the man's directions. He speaks, "To get home, you must turn you truck around. Go to the fork in the road, take the left fork. This will lead you to Bolombo. After you pass Bolombo, you will come to the ferry at Lodi. Take the road from Lodi to Mushenge. From Mushenge, go to Bulape. From Bulape, you can work your way back to Kananga."

A trip of 60 miles. Now 60 miles in the city can take somewhere in the neighborhood of 45 minutes – depending on how we drive! For some it is longer, for others obviously it takes less time! We will not go into that at this point. In the forest, to go 60 miles, meant that Bill and his companion would drive throughout the night, past breakfast and lunch the next day, and not arrive home until almost suppertime.

Thinking very much about what and where the Lord is, Bill lets out a deep sigh, turns his truck around and heads off into the African forest.

Now, what about you? We know that the disciples are where God wants them, doing what the Lord wants them to do. We know the same thing about Bill Washburn. What about you? Are you living your life doing what the Lord wants you to do, or just living? Did you take that job because everyone expected you to? Did you marry him because you were expected to do so? Are you acting 70 years old because everyone expects you to act 70 years old? What about your life?

Aside from those of you who are trapped in some self-destructive horrible sin, this is a question that rarely crosses our minds. If we could visit briefly, you would probably say something like, "Well, Ben, I guess I never really thought about it. My life is okay. I go to work and I have my family. There is not a whole lot going on. I guess it is okay with the Lord," and that would be that.

However, on those rare occasions when I can spend some time with you, I am amazed at my findings. It never ceases to surprise me to hear the things shared around a campfire, a quail field, or on someone's front porch. It usually begins the same way. "Ben, I guess my life is okay. I go to work and I do my job. But, Ben, you know there are times........." or, "Ben, if I have to go to that dumb office one more day......." or, "Ben, if he treats me like that in public one more time......." or perhaps, most painfully of all, "Ben, if I have to wake up and be old and alone one more day......... I just do not know what I am going to do."

Do you ever feel that way? Do you ever feel like just chunking it and disappearing? If you do, then rejoice. Do you know what that means? It means that you are not dead yet. You are still alive and there is something within that is pushing you on! Look at the disciples. They were where the Lord wanted them and doing what the Lord wanted them to do – "but some doubted."

Travel in Zaire is very difficult. The roads are extremely rough and comprised mainly with sand. The vehicles are all diesel powered. They have that sort of diesel smell to them. You roll up the windows zoom into a trip because the dust gets in your eyes, nose and clings to your teeth. You are clipping along at a brisk 3-4 miles per hour. Conversation disappears quickly. Ultimately, you simply struggle to find a way to hold on and protect your back from the constant pounding. The hours drag by.

Darkness comes rapidly. The trees reach across the dirt road to form a canopy shielding you from the stars. There are no streetlights. There are no other vehicles on the road. The only light besides your headlights is an occasional campfire in a nearby village. The campfires are extinguished rather early. Families go into their huts at night. You are alone.

Time passed slowly. At around 11:00 p.m., Bill Washburn and his companion realized that they were in a part of the forest they had never seen before that evening. As midnight approached, they came around another curve in the forest road, and their headlights hit upon a figure in the road. Rather than run over the person, he stopped the truck. His headlights were shining on the tallest woman he had ever seen in Africa. She was wearing a hooded robe. It reached all the way to the ground. Her arms were outstretched and every bit of exposed skin was painted white.

Before he could say anything to his companion, the truck was surrounded by a crowd of people wearing white robes and painted white. They opened the doors of the truck. They helped your missionary and his companion out of the truck. They were pushed off the side of the road and forced to walk into the forest.

In the distance, they heard drums beating. As they moved along, they became aware of the smell of torches burning. The drums grew louder. The smoke from the diesel soaked rag torches grew stronger in their nostrils. They came to a clearing and were stunned at the sight. Part of the forest had been cleared away. Torches were lit and arranged in a large circle. In the center of the circle was one large stake going straight up in the air. It looked like a setting for a ceremonial sacrifice!

Consider all of these things, and then tell me that you have doubts in your life? As Bill told me this part of the story, I looked at him in amazement and exclaimed, "Bill, what in the world did you do?" Bill looked at me and responded, "Why Ben, I prayed. I prayed."

I do not know about you, but when my life hits some part of the jungle I have never been in before, one of the first things I forget to do is pray! When I am confronted with a crisis, a sickness, or something I have never experienced before, if I pray at all, I might have prayed, "Lord, I hope my buddy makes it to the truck because I am gone!"

However, since Bill Washburn was simply where God wanted him to be, doing what the Lord wanted him to do, even with his doubts, he could claim the next verse of scripture! "All authority in heaven and on earth has been given to me."

What of your life? During periods of introspection, do you find that you failed to abdicate the throne of your existence? Are you still seated at the center of your own life, or have you yielded all to Jesus Christ? Twentieth Century believers often fail to recognize that the same authority given to the first disciples in Christ is given also to us. As Christians, we are not only called to accept Christ as Savior of our lives, but as Lord of our very being as well. To allow Christ to become the center of our lives is to tap into the wellspring of His eternal authority.

The early translators of scripture understood that we can generally resist anything but temptation. No sooner do we turn something over to the Lord, then we take it back. We continue to desperately attempt to retain control over our lives when Christ calls us to constant brokenness. To be broken is to realize that in and of our own power we are incapable of doing anything pleasing in the sight of God. When we attempt to control the lives of those around us or our own lives, we stand between the Lord and His graceful desires for each of us. I sincerely believe that is why the Great Commandment was included in this text. As I am dictating this chapter, I am driving down the highway in Atlanta. I have just seen an excellent example of today's selfishness. A car just passed me with a license plate that read JST4ME, "Just for Me." What an accurate description of today's spiritual condition. When all of society is built around individual hedonism, it makes it very difficult for the Christian to understand that we are called to give our lives away for Christ.

The Great Commandment is often emphasized from the standpoint of the going instead of the doing. The imperative in the passage is found in the making of disciples, not in the going. Jesus offers willing disciples an imperative affirmation, not direction. He recognizes that if we were all where He wants us, and doing what He wants us to do, then marching orders are not in order! Rather, His Holy Spirit fills our heart as a heavenly cheerleader – urging us on to make disciples of all nations!

What about Bill? You recall the setting. The drums are pounding. The smoke from the torches is burning his nostrils. He is surrounded by a great crowd of witnesses wearing their dress whites. The drums abruptly stopped.

The crowd falls silent. The woman who met him on the road stands before your missionary and speaks, "We knew you were coming tonight." Bill responds, "You could not have known that I was coming tonight. I have come this way only because of a detour. The bridge was washed away and I was forced to come this route. You could not have known I was coming this way." "We serve the Unknown God. He told us that you were coming tonight and would tell us His name. Tell us, who is the Unknown God?"

And because Bill Washburn was simply where God wanted him, doing what the Lord wanted him to do, even in a time of doubt, he had the wonderful, glorious privilege of leading an entire tribe of people to a saving knowledge of Jesus Christ! Ultimately, he had the opportunity to baptize them in the name of the Father and of the Son and of the Holy Spirit. Ultimately, he had the opportunity to teach them of the commandments of Jesus Christ. Wow! If that does not give you goose bumps, then perhaps you are dead.

He went on to be a General in the Army. However, during World War II, he was Colonel Creighton Abrams. The story is told that Colonel Abrams was a battalion commander in Europe during the war. One evening he was awakened by his officers with the news that his battalion was trapped. They were completely surrounded by the enemy. In the face of this predicament, Colonel Abrams called his officers together and said, "Gentlemen, for the first time in the history of this campaign, we are in a position to strike the enemy from any direction." What a wonderful outlook on life! I want you to realize something – for the first time in the history of the Church, we are finally in a position to walk out the doors of your church, go in any direction we choose, and attack the enemies of the Lord. We can go in any direction and attack the enemies of disease, ignorance, voodoo, witchcraft, famine, substance abuse, physical abuse, corrupt governments, and oppression and we will win! We will win with men and women who are willing to examine their lives. We will win with men and women prepared to take a step if need be. We will win with men and women prepared to allow Christ to be the center of their existence.

The word of God calls you to examine your life. It calls us to examine our lives not only in relation to the mission to the Church, but relative to our everyday existence as well. Therefore, I end this chapter by encouraging you to spend some time alone with the Lord. As you look within, you should find that Christ is not the center of your life, I beg you, move over. Give Christ the throne. For some, that is a very difficult proposition. For some, it means facing the necessity of forgiveness. For others, it will end your right to be bitter or petty. For others, it may call forth a new commitment to Christ and the work of His Church. Regardless, as you take your steps, recall the words of our Lord when He said, "Lo, I am with you always, to the end of the age.

Three Words

Exodus 8

"Then the Lord said to Moses, "Go to Pharaoh and say to him, 'This is what the Lord says: Let my people go, so that they may worship me. If your refuse to let them go, I will plague your whole country with frogs. The river shall swarm with frogs. They shall come up into your palace, into your bed chamber and into your bed and into the houses of your people, and into your ovens and your kneading bowls. The frogs shall come up on you and your people and on all your officials'."

I am going to read something to you. It is from a treasure of mine. It is a tiny little book that was given to me by Captain Luke McConnell. Luke was the commanding officer of Kilo Company, the Three One Marines in Haditha, Iraq. My son was his executive officer and many of you will recall that I was imbedded with that company of Marines for a month and had a chance to be with my son in war. That would have been quite a Father's Day gift, I guess you could say.

To thank us for coming, Luke gave me this little book and this is a page out of it. It is a talk that was given by a man named Theodore Roosevelt a hundred years ago called "The Strenuous Life." Listen to just a little of it.

"Far better it is to dare mighty things. To win glorious triumphs, even though checkered by failure, than to take rank with those poor spirits who neither enjoy much nor suffer much because they live in the great twilight that knows not victory nor defeat."

I will read that to you again, but I will start at the head of the paragraph because it makes more sense.

"As it is with the individual, so it is with the nation and with the church. Far better it is to dare mighty things. To win glorious triumphs, even though checkered by failure, than to take rank with those poor spirits who neither enjoy much nor suffer much because they live in the great twilight that knows not victory nor defeat."

Hmmmm. I am an American. I am a Southern American. I am a desperate Presbyterian Patriot and I work overseas. I come back to this country and I read the same newspapers you read, I watch the same television, I listen to the same news, and I am pretty convinced that there are a whole bunch of us in the church and in this country at large who are suffering from a disease that I have labeled Pharaohitis.

You know the story. People of Israel are being held captive by Pharaoh. Moses goes to Pharaoh, what does he say? "Let my people go." Pharaoh says, "I am not going to do it." What does Moses do? He turns the Nile River into blood. That was the first curse. A week later he comes back to Pharaoh and says "Set my people free." Pharaoh says, "I'm not going to do it." Moses then covers the land with frogs. Now that is the part that we just read. What you didn't read was what happens after that. Go back to your text and look at verse 10, because Moses goes back to Pharaoh and he asks one of the most important questions of all time. Moses goes to Pharaoh and says, "When do you want the frogs to go away?" In verse 10, Pharaoh answers him and says, "Tomorrow." Tomorrow. Tomorrow. Do you get it? Pharaoh wants to spend another night with the frogs.

Now, y'all, I'm from Tennessee. I like frogs just as much as the next guy, but in the bed with you? You are going to take a shower and there are frogs in the shower and in your kitchen. You see Pharaoh had just gotten so accustomed to things being just awful. It was not just Israel, it was not just Moses, and everything was just awful. Pharaoh had gotten so used to things being awful that if it all went away he would not know what to do about it. Pharaohitis is that disease that we get when we are so constantly bombarded with nothing but bad news about the war, about the economy, about the administration, about the society, about the church. We are so bombarded with bad news that if it all went away and things were fine, we would not know what to do.

This morning we are going to do something pretty important. First, we are going to have a little self-diagnosis to find out if in fact, you are suffering from this malady. But here is the good news. If you discover that you are in fact suffering from Pharaohitis, praise the Lord, today in this place we are having a healing service. You can be set free from Pharaohitis and start life all over again. Say amen. Amen.

Now, here is the first question. Don't raise your hand. Don't say it out loud. Would you rather worship or whine? Would you rather celebrate or complain? Did you wake up this morning going "Oh Lord!" or did you go "Oh Looooorrrrd." What about the last five phone calls you made? Were they to build someone up and say something good or were you complaining? Your last five emails; were you gossiping or were you saying something good about someone? I can see some elbows doing this. You know who I am talking to. You know, if you find that you have Pharaohitis, it is okay. Like I said, you can be healed today in this place and it begins when you remember something very simple. God loves you, so much. Let's just stop right there. God loves you so much. We could call the dogs and go home, but let's don't. But when you remember that God loves you so much that three thousand years ago he whispered into the ear of a man named David and he said, "David, write this down, so they will never forget." David wrote,

> "The Lord is my shepherd; I shall not want. He makes me lie down in green pastures, He leads me beside still waters, and He restores my soul. He leads me into the paths of righteousness for His name sake. Yeah, though I walk through the valley of the shadow of death, I will fear no evil for Thou art with me; Thy rod and Thy staff, they comfort me. Thou

> preparest a table before me in the presence of mine enemies, Thou anoint my head with oil; my cup runneth over. Surely goodness and mercy shall follow me all the days of my life, and I will dwell in the house of the Lord forever."

How many of you have ever heard that before? Raise your hands. Good for you. How many of you have memorized them? Raise them up. You know memorizing God's word is a wonderful, wonderful thing. It means in times of trouble, God's word will bubble up in your heart, but it can also mean that God's word can become rote. In a few minutes we are going to say *The Apostles' Creed*. The next time you are stuck out in Highland and you get caught in traffic, try to say *The Apostles' Creed*. It is really kind of hard to do. God's word can do a lot of things.

John and I have a friend, we both know who it is, we are not going to say it out loud, but we have a friend who is a pastor and when he comes to call on people like you and you are not home, he will take his business card and leave it in the door. That way you know he came by to see you and he gets some brownie points. Well to seem religious, our friend always writes a Bible verse on his business card and usually he writes Revelations 3:20, "Behold I stand at the door and knock."

He did that until he got his business card back in the offering plate and on the backside someone had written Genesis 3:10, "I heard you in the garden and I hid because I was naked."

We are not going to do that with God's word this morning, but we are going to have some fun with it. I want to tell you what I have been doing with God's word for the last 15 months of my life because that is really when it started getting tough. Now, I do not know what you do. I do not know how it comes over you, but if I have this feeling of defeat or worry or fear that wants to creep up in me; in my life it starts kind of like a storm on the horizon. You sort of see the clouds coming. It just does not all of a sudden fall on me like this thing with a wham and you're defeated and feel awful. It just does not happen that way. For me, it just sort of boils up really slow and what I have been doing for the last 15 months; when I start feeling fear or worry or concern for the ministry, for the country, for my family, for any these things, right out loud, right out loud, I start saying "Thank you Jesus. Thank you Jesus. Thank you Jesus." Say that with me…. Thank you Jesus. One more time, I can't hear you…. Thank you Jesus.

I keep saying "Thank you Jesus" until my praises are louder than my pessimism and then I remember that the praises go up and the blessings come down and all that pessimism goes away. Let me just tell you, if you struggle with that in life about these days. You do that. The next time you start to slide and feel down in the dumps, right out loud, say "Thank you Jesus".

Then I have taken the 23rd Psalm and about 15 months ago I decided to make the 23rd Psalm a part of my life. That means that I say it right out loud when I'm lying in bed in the morning. Half way through the day I am going to one meeting or another and I am in traffic in Atlanta or some other city, or anywhere in the world, and I will say the 23rd Psalm right out loud. Again, in the afternoon, before I go to bed I say it and I have built it into my life so that in difficult times it becomes a part of who I am.

I was on the Kukra River down in Nicaragua. It is a little jungle river that is probably as wide as the church is long. It is not real big. It is a brand new boat. A brand new engine. We have about 15 people in the boat. We have gone from Blue Fields all the way up the river to a place called San Francisco and we did revival services, had a big day, it's late in the day, we are zooming down this jungle river, it is so much fun, and my brand new, did I say it was brand new? My brand new engine goes Phhhhhhh and that's it. Now I don't know if you know this or not, but when it gets dark on a little jungle river, the jungle reaches across the river and sort of closes down on top of you and every creature in the jungle comes to life all at once. Everyone is screaming and hollering in the jungle and I look around at my friends, and I have some little kids on this boat, it is dark and it's late in the night and they are getting very scared and right out loud I just said "The Lord is my shepherd and everything is going to be alright."

We started reaching around in our pockets and everyone found they had their cell phones. Hallelujah! We turned on the cell phones and not a one of them worked in the jungle and then for some reason I remembered I had packed a satellite phone. Hallelujah, we are going to be okay. I raised the antenna, turned on the satellite phone, and the country code for Nicaragua is 505. Well I discovered if I dialed 505 in Nicaragua I get some guy in Northern New Mexico who was not happy that I woke him up in the middle of the night. So I am thinking how are we going to get home? Then I decide to call my best friend in Atlanta and I am going to ask him to call someone in Nicaragua to come down the coast and up the river and find us so we will live happily ever after. So, it's about 2:00 in the morning and I call my best friend, Dr. Chris Price, also a pastor. "Hey Chris, this is Ben. I am broken down on a river in Nicaragua." Chris said, "Well of course you are. Why else would you call me?" "I just wanted to say hello and I need a little help." "Of course you do. What can I do for you?" And bless his heart, my SAT phone is to my ear, Chris has one phone on his ear and takes the other phone that he has and you can hear him calling my friend about 50 miles away in Blue Fields. He wakes up Juan at 2:00 in the morning who gets in a boat and comes down the coast and up the river, rescues us, and we live happily ever after, because the Lord is my shepherd and everything is going to be alright.

In November of 2007, Iran landed troops on the coast of Nicaragua at a place called Monkey Point. They declared to the people of Monkey Point, Nicaragua that they were going to kick them off their land, spend $350 million dollars, dig a deep water port on the coast of Nicaragua, and put a canal across the country and open an embassy in Managua, the capital city. That came out in our news one day and one day only, December 17, 2007. December 18, 2007, I had my tickets to Nicaragua. The only reason in the world that I can imagine that Iran would come to our side of the world is because they want to learn about Jesus.

Doesn't that make sense to you? Say amen. Of course it does.

So I ordered a whole bunch of our digital solar-powered Bibles in Farsi, their language. I could not go until February, but in February, Dr. Chris Price, the fellow I woke up in the middle of the night, joined me. We flew to Managua and I decided that I would go find Akbar Ishmail Pour, their Ambassador. Let's start right at the top. I went to the Iranian Embassy and they had closed it, so I thought well if I was from Iran and I was hiding in Managua, where would I hide? I would hide in the Venezuelan Embassy; they don't like us either. I went running into the Venezuelan Embassy going, "Is Akbar here? I have a meeting with him and I am running late." The lady at the desk said, "No, but he will be back in an hour." I found him!

I gave Bibles in Spanish to all the Venezuelans, they are precious Christian people, and then I took a big piece of paper and I wrote:

> "Dear Akbar, here is the Bible you wanted."

And I left it out in public. We flew across the country and went down from Blue Fields and took a boat down the coast of Nicaragua to Monkey Point and met with the precious Christian people of Monkey Point, Nicaragua. They speak English and they speak Spanish. They are Creole people. Incredibly strong people. We talked about what does it feel like to be threatened on your own land, to be kicked off your own land, to be forced to convert to another religion if you want a job, and if you get a job, it's digging ditches, how does that make you feel? And they did not like it.

We shared our Bibles with them. They are all Christian people. They thought these were the neatest things in the world and they wanted to know how they could share the gospel with the 42 Iranian Revolutionary Guard soldiers who had landed a helicopter in their village. We just happened to have some Farsi Bibles with us. We gave them to the courageous Christians of Monkey Point and when Iran came back and landed their helicopter at Monkey Point, the people of Monkey Point met the Iranian Revolutionary Guard troops with Bibles in hand, gave them to the soldiers, and said you go listen to this and then come back and talk to us and they kicked them out of the village of Monkey Point. Say amen! That's courage.

Iran goes on the radio in Nicaragua and says they are displeased with me. Ahhhhh. In the meantime, we have rebuilt their churches, added sidewalks, water systems, redone the school. I want you to see pictures of this. Their big sport is Knot Soccer. You have to come and see the Monkey Point Stars, my team. It is so much fun. These are such wonderful people. This goes on over a period of almost a year and a half since I have seen you last. I go back down to lead revival services in Monkey Point concerned that the government of Nicaragua is not necessarily on our side and they told me I had to go on a Monday and come back on a Wednesday to Monkey Point and I thought that was so odd. I decided I would go on a Tuesday and come back on a Thursday.

Oh, we went down, had revival services, a great time was had by all, neat people, and I feel like part of the family in Monkey Point. Early in the morning we had to come back up the coast. My government has told me the danger I am in is the 35 miles from Monkey Point to Blue Fields is nothing but open ocean and jungle and that is where I will meet Iran and that is their fear for me.

You know how the ocean is just perfectly flat early in the mornings; it's like a pane of glass? We are in that same brand new boat (we fixed the engine), still brand new boat, brand new engine. We are zooming up the coast of Nicaragua. It is pitch black dark. When it gets to where you can just begin to see the outline of things, we look out into the ocean and as far as you can see, the sky is one huge boiling thunderstorm. This is very dangerous in an open boat out in the ocean. In fact, two weeks earlier, some of the folks of Monkey Point lost their lives in a storm just like this. We can see the storm coming and right out loud, I said, "Yeah, though we walk through the valley of the shadow of death, we are not going to be afraid of a thing and in the name of Jesus, storm you be gone!"

Now can you remember being little and getting tickled in church or tickled in school and you wanted to laugh so bad you couldn't stand it, but if you did you would get in trouble? You remember that feeling? You tried to hold it in and you just thought you were going to explode? Do what you want to with this, rays of light started bursting through this storm! It looked like something out of a movie and as the rays of light came through that storm and as it broke up right in front of us, you could feel that everyone in the boat just to explode laughing, but no one wanted to be the first to do it and finally someone got tickled and folks started waving their hands and we started singing hymns. We were watching the storm just fall apart in front of our eyes. We were just laughing at the top of our lungs and we got drenched because we did not see the storm coming in from behind us and it rolled right over us!

When it happened, Willie, my staff director, looked at me and said it means our problems are not coming from the ocean, they are coming from the jungle and we had better get out of here. We took our boat and we dove up a tiny jungle river and we worked our way back to Blue Fields. We never ran into Iran and we lived to fight another day because even though we walked through the valley of the shadow, the Lord was with us even then.

Then it says, "Surely goodness and mercy shall follow me all the days of my life." Not just 18 months ago when the economy was okay, but even now? Is that what it means? Does it mean next week when things might get worse? Two weeks from now? Goodness and mercy. Goodness is God's greatest desire. Goodness is God's greatest desire which is because of Jesus Christ, God wants to bless you. That's what goodness is. God wants to bless you with a sense of peace, security, health, strength, and prosperity. Goodness is God's greatest desire which is to bless you because of Jesus Christ. Mercy is when God goes to all this trouble to bless you and you don't even say, "Thank you Jesus" and he loves you anyway. I will tell you that again.

Goodness is God's greatest desire, which is to bless you in good times, bad times, horrible times, and frightening times. God's greatest desire is to bless you and part of that is peace, part of that is prosperity. Mercy is when God goes to all the trouble to bless you and you don't even say "thank you" and he loves you anyway.

I told you I am going to give you three words that will change your life.... I guess it is really six. "Thank you Jesus" would be the first three. Here's the next two. These two words can change your life if you are living with Pharaohitis. If you were living in that grey twilight that knows not victory nor defeat, then you take the word "If" and you take the word "then" and you add it to the 23rd Psalm and say it to yourself:

> *"If the Lord is my shepherd, then I shall not want. If the Lord is my shepherd, and then even if I am in the valley of the shadow of death, I don't need to be afraid. If the Lord is my shepherd, then everything is going to be alright. Thank you Jesus."*

Build that into your life. The third word is the tough one. The first two are easy. If and then are fun. It's that last word that makes this so difficult. "Is". Is the Lord your shepherd or are you trying to do it all? Is the Lord your shepherd or would you rather sit and worry? If the Lord your shepherd or would you rather whine than worship? Is the Lord your shepherd or would you rather complain than celebrate? You are the only one that can answer that. Is the Lord your shepherd or are you trying to get through these times on your own?

If you are an elder in this church, will you raise your hand for me really quick? I want everyone in this church to look at the hands that are raised around you right now and I want to tell you about those folks. Those are people who will kneel with you, wherever you need to pray. Those are people who will stand with you, wherever you need to stand. Those are people who will walk with you, wherever you need to go. If it helps you understand that the Lord is my shepherd. The Lord is your shepherd and because of that, everything is going to be alright.

I told you I'm from Tennessee. I'm from Memphis. Did you know I spent three and one-half years in prison? Did y'all know that about me? A lot of you knew that already. Watch my lips. I was a law enforcement Chaplain in Memphis. I could leave any time I wanted to. Does everyone understand that? Back in 1974, I had an inmate who was part of a team of guys and we rewrote the book of Psalms into prison jive and my friend, Cadillac Cookie, rewrote the 23rd Psalm for me in 1974 and I want you to hear it.

> *"The Lord is my leader and everything's cool. He lets me crash in the green grass. He guides me besides the resting waters. He guides me down the roads of righteousness in his honor, dig this, as I stroll through the valley of the shadow of death, I will back off no evil for we art together. Thy rod and staff have all my slack. Thou set up a table in front of me around those that don't dig me.*

> *Thou layeth the oil upon my head. I am cool and comfortable. I'm hip. That goodness and mercy shall follow me all the days of my life and I will be a guest in the crib of the Lord from now on."*
> *Amen.*

Christian, I say to you this day, if in the moment of honesty that we allow ourselves to be ourselves, if you find in these tough times that you are living in that grey twilight, which knows no victory nor defeat, the cure for Pharaohitis is very simple. Lift up your praises and say "Thank you Jesus." As the praises go up, the blessings come down. And add "if" and "then" to the 23rd Psalm and find that "if" the Lord is your shepherd, then oh dear Christian, everything is going to be alright.

If you need to take a step closer to Jesus, you saw people that raised their hands, you also know that I'm here and John's here, and in the name of Christ, we hold our hand to you and say in the name of Jesus, come on home, everything's going to be alright. For that I am grateful and I hope you are too. You stay strong and God Bless America!

Remember Who You Are!
2 Timothy 1:3-7

"I thank God whom I serve with a clear conscience, as did my fathers, when I remember you constantly in my prayers. As I remember you tears, I long night and day to see you, that I may be filled with joy. I am reminded of your sincere faith, a faith that dwelt first in your grandmother Lois and your mother Eunice, and now, I am sure dwells in you. Hence, I remind you to rekindle the gift of God that is within you through the laying on of my hands; for God did not give us the spirit of timidity, but a spirit of power and love and self-control."

I have certainly enjoyed sharing my thoughts with you. This has been an interesting discipline for me, and I certainly hope you have been inspired by the stories and Biblical insights I have offered. However, I wish this book was over! I wish you could put this book down, walk to your mailbox, and instead, receive a letter from me. I would title that letter, "Remember Who You Are!" Now that is not a new idea at all. You see, that is what Paul is doing with Brother Timothy. Brother Timothy is our final text.

Brother Timothy was a whole lot like a whole lot of us. He took seriously his relationship with Jesus Christ. He also was concerned with the needs of everyday life. We do not know if Timothy had a family or not, but we know that he was certainly kept busy by his calling in life. In addition, Paul had placed a burden upon Timothy's heart. Timothy was not only concerned with his personal spiritual growth, but was concerned also with the well-being of Christians in the known world.

He lived in a day that was very much like our own. In Timothy's day, the economy was shot to pieces. In our day, we do not what is going to happen! In Timothy's day, morals had hit an all-time low. Martin Luther wrote of the days and said, "Vices were being worn into people, not worn out of people!" In Timothy's day, the church was rampantly persecuted. In our times, it is a much subtler form of persecution. In these days, the church is persecuted by distraction. As everyone knows, it is a closer drive to the lake than to the church or any given summer Sunday morning!

With all of these distractions, it becomes obvious why it is so easy to simply, "Find our spot in a pew" and not budge! It is so easy to want to throw our hands up and say, "Lord, I am here, but don't challenge me. Lord, I am here, but don't stretch my faith. Lord, I am simply a disenchanted disciple. I will do all that I can, but never expect that to be so very much."

I cannot help but suppose that Timothy had become something of a disenchanted disciple. Perhaps that is why Paul wrote him the letter that I wish I could write to each of you, including myself!

I would start my letter to each of you the same way Paul did. "I thank God when I remember you in my prayers. I remember your tears and I long to be with you that I may be filled with joy!" Now, no one is going to cry when this book is over. However, I feel confident that some of you have been moved with tears of compassion at the stories you have read. I am certain that the suffering of this world has been made real to you in this text and that you would like to do something about it. To those of you who fit that description, I could begin my letter the same way Paul began his to Timothy. I do long to be with people who want to change the world for Jesus Christ!

Where was Paul when he wrote this letter? If you don't know the answer, simply say "jail". If you ever wonder about the whereabouts of Paul, he was usually locked up somewhere! Many of you are aware that I spent 3-1/2 years as a law enforcement Chaplain. I want to make something perfectly clear. I could leave anytime I wanted to! I was not locked up; I was a Chaplain. I want to submit a thought to you. It is my best guess that inmates in Paul's time were not very different from inmates today. With this in mind, imagine the following scenario:

Paul is trying to grab Timothy's attention. He is using the written word and inspired as it may be, he wants to say something very powerful. He has his stylus poised over the papyrus and he pauses. At the instant of that pause an inmate we will name Augustine leans forward and says something to an inmate we will call Octavus. They immediately come to blows. Paul is astonished by this violence and reflects upon it. What did the first inmate say? Something rather unpleasant about the family of the second inmate, specifically his mother! I don't know how many times I have seen inmates get into a fight over what someone else called someone else's momma!

Paul is flabbergasted, picks up his stylus and writes, "I remember the faith not only of your grandmother, but of your mother as well and I am sure that faith dwells in you too!"

Paul is simply saying to Timothy and he is saying to each of us, "Look as you look at your life, REMEMBER WHO YOU ARE! You are the people of God, who come from a long line of believers. Your history, your heritage, your roots are grounded in the fact that you are the people of God."

Think about that for a moment. Think back over your life, to someone very special. I want you to remember that person that you know struggled so desperately, but always exemplified a magnificent Christian faith. Was it your mother or grandmother? Was it a pastor or perhaps your father? Regardless, when we consider what others have had to bear, it can be pretty embarrassing. I know that I look at the things that tripped me up, and compared to the sufferings of others, I have favored very poorly. Paul says to Timothy and he says to you, "As you look at your life, remember that you are of the people of God – who had all the trials and the struggles and the hardships and the jobs, but believers!" Then see if you do not hear way off in the distance somewhere, "Faith of our fathers living still in spite of dungeon, fire, sword, the economy, the loneliness of age, the temptations of youth, parents that are driving you crazy, children that are driving you crazy, a marriage that is on its knees, Timothy, remember who you are!"

Am I Ever Going to Get Out of Here?

Once we remember our heritage, Paul tells us to do something about it. "Rekindle that gift of God that is within you." It is really so very obvious. If you are a believer in Jesus Christ, then do not be afraid to smile about it!

As you know, I enjoy hunting and fishing all over the United States. As I travel, I have had the wonderful blessing of meeting some very unusual people around the world. On a recent hunting trip to South Georgia, I met an elderly woman who made quite a pronouncement. She said, "If you've got good news in your heart, then you ought to notify your face!" I love that! Let's expand it. If you have good news in your heart:

>Notify your heart and smile.

>Notify your body and serve.

>Notify your heart and love.

>Notify your wallet and give!

Never be afraid of doing something good for the Lord.

Why? Because God has equipped you to meet the challenge before us. "For God did not give us the spirit of timidity...." Timidity is not a bad translation. That implies meekness or shyness. It paints the picture of someone who hangs their head and shuffles their feet. However, more literally the word means cowardice. Paul is saying to Timothy and he is saying to you – God did not call you to face your life as a coward. At its worst, being a coward means letting the world roll right over you. At its best, being a coward means that you face life simply holding your own. I do not believe either.

Harry Emerson Fosdick said it so well, "There is nothing more impressive than courage. Fighting with the scabbard, once the sword is gone." I wish someone would needlepoint that for me. What have you lost in life? Did you get caught? Did you get away with it? Did someone call you a name and you never got over it? Did someone that you love leave you? Did someone die that you believed would always be there for you? Are you trying to take what is left of life and make the most of it? Well Timothy, because of Jesus Christ, you have the right to take the rest of your life and claim it as a victory for Him! Even if it did not begin until just now, you have the right to recognize that you are accepted, secure, loved, and forgiven in Jesus Christ. There is great strength in those words and Timothy, if you will let them sink in, they very well may change your life as you REMEMBER WHO YOU ARE!

There are times, when each of us feels as if we cannot go on any further. In those times, claim for yourself the knowledge that God has equipped you to do something about your life. God has given to you His very own spirit of power, love, and self-control.

In certain parts of the country, the economy of our nation is still quite depressed. If you are not involved in the particular industry that is booming, you are involved in a part of the economy that is suffering desperately. In one portion of the south, I have a friend whose business is richly blessed. He had an opportunity to travel to Europe with his family for six months. During this trip, he was going to promote his business and see all the sights of that magnificent land. While he was gone, he wanted to do a good deed. Let's call my friend Bill. I will let him tell the story from this point.

"I met with one of the local builders. I told him I know that times have been tough in the building industry. I want you to know that I have an opportunity to go on a long and very profitable trip. While I am gone, I want you to build me a house. Here are the plans to the house. Here is the money to build this house. Now, if you will, build me this house while I am gone. I want you to use the very best of everything in its construction. I want you to use the best carpet and the best light fixtures. Use the best plumbing and wiring. Use the best insulation and roofing. You use the best of everything, but build me that house, okay?

Well the builder went to work. He got the foundation of the house completed and was beginning work on the sub-flooring. A thought crossed his mind that one grade of sub-flooring was just like another. There would be no way to tell if he had used the best grade or not. Needless to say, he did not use the best grade, took a little money off the top, and put it in his pocket. When it came time to work on the wiring and plumbing the same thoughts crossed his mind. He took a little more money off the top, and put it in his pocket. The builder got on a roll and he cut every corner he could, but he built that house. When I returned I met the builder and he said, 'Well, sir, here are the keys to your house.' I responded, "I appreciate that. I want you to know that times have been tough in your industry. I know you have a great big family and I wanted to give you a job. That is why I had you build this house. However, I also wanted to do a good deed. I want you to know that I had you build this house for you and your own family. Here are the keys back. That is the best house you'll ever deserve!"

For the rest of his life, that builder will live in a house that he knows is second rate. Well, Timothy, do you see that spirit of self-control? More literally translated, it is the spirit of ability to do all things right and properly in the name of Jesus Christ. Timothy, as you live your life, remember who you are!

Underneath the spirit of ability to act properly, God has also given you His spirit of love. It is agape, the unconditional, unselfish love of God in Jesus Christ. It is that love that takes hands and hearts that are closed to the world and opens them to everyone. It is that love that enables us to do far more than we ever imagined. Timothy, you possess that love!

If you are like most Christians, you are about to quit reading. Don't you do that! You are so close to the end of this book, do not put it down! As believers in Christ, we do not mind thinking of ourselves as ethical and relatively loving. Those are fine qualities that free us from a lot of other faults and responsibilities. However, most of us do not enjoy entertaining the possibility that we are proprietors of God's very own spirit of power. That would necessitate a response. Interjecting God's power into our lives means that there is the distinct possibility that God can use us to play some part in changing the world for Christ and we do not like it! Oh, it's fine for the past to be used by God. It is fine for the choir and the choir director to be used by God, but it is not fine to imagine God using me. I am the one who lost his word, remember me?

I spoke in my hometown of Memphis. Tennessee. After the meeting, a gentleman came to me and asked what he could do to help. He stated that he was not a physician, but that he wanted to send me some of his product. Without much thought, I agreed.

Do you have a convenience store in your neighborhood? They go by many names, Magic Mart, 7-11, etc. Within each of those fine little stores, there is an unusually large candy counter. Row after row of mints, suckers, candy bars, and chewing gum greet each shopper. So often, the temptation is more than they can resist. I am amazed that such items are left out in the open and actually believe that candy bars and such temptations should be placed somewhere behind the counter. Nevertheless, on your next visit to such a convenience store, notice the smell of the candy counter. It has a very distinct odor that can be found nowhere else in the world. The man in Memphis responded. It turns out he works for a company that makes bubble gum! He sent me 300 pounds of bubble gum and my entire house smelled like a convenience store candy counter! The bubble gum came in 25 pound boxes. Attempting to be as helpful as possible, I sent 25 pound boxes of bubble gum to physicians who were preparing to visit various mission fields. I received a phone call from Dr. Frank Hellinger of Orlando, Florida. The phone conversation went something like this:

"Mathes, what is this stuff?" said the irate physician.

"Frank what does it look like?" I responded as gently as possible.

"It looks like bubble gum."

"That is good, Frank. You are a smart man! If I ever get sick, I'm going to come and see you!"

Frank said, "Well, what am I supposed to do with this?"

"Frank, why not take it to Africa and give it to the little children?"

"I am not going to Africa to give out bubble gum to a bunch of children – harrumph, harrumph, and harrumph!" End of conversation.

Dr. Hellinger went to Zaire and served at the Good Shepherd Hospital. Whenever he went his lab jacket was filled with bubble gum. He delighted in sharing it with the children! They called it "boom boom." Each morning the little children would gather outside the guesthouse at the Good Shepherd Hospital. Upon seeing the good doctor, they would jump up and down asking for their daily treat!

Dr. Hellinger is a very fine physician. He noticed a little boy that walked differently than the other children. He knew right away that this young man had a tumor growing on his spine. We don't have a lot of fancy tools at our hospital in Zaire. If he attempted to operate on the little boy and made a mistake the little boy would be paralyzed. If he chose not to operate on the little boy, the little boy would end up paralyzed. He chose to operate.

Dr. Hellinger spent four hours getting to the tumor. He arrived safely, but he found that the little boy needed a pint of blood. We had no refrigeration in those days. You did not simply walk down the hall and pick up a pint of plasma. They went to the little boy's mother who had abandoned her child on the operating table. She believed that if she gave blood to her son and he died, she would die too.

Flossie Hellinger spoke up, "Frank, I have A-positive blood. You give him every drop of mine, but you keep that little boy alive!" Frank is very good. He took one pint from his wife, Flossie, and stabilized the young man's condition. He returned to surgery and four hours later managed to safely remove the tumor from the little boy's spine. The child was going to be just fine!

The little boy needed another pint of blood. While still wearing his mask, gown, cap, gloves, and boots, Dr. Hellinger walked out of the operating room and paraded through the waiting area, hitting his arm and shouting, "A-positive blood! A-positive blood!" He told me later that people got up and walked away. They would not look him in the eye. They bent over and tied shoes they were not even wearing. When he had reached the end of his rope, he remembered that box of bubble gum. He ran back to the guesthouse and came back with his treasure. Placing the bubble gum on a patient cart, he wheeled through the waiting area shouting, "A-positive blood, boom boom. A-positive blood, boom boom!" After an eternity, a man came forward and swapped a pint of blood for two large scoops of bubble gum.

Frank returned to the operating room and guess what? That little boy was fine. I have played soccer with him, and by the way, that other fellow has a mouth full of cavities! If you are a dentist and reading this book, get in touch with me! We have some dental work to perform!

So many Christians these days have a tendency to take the obvious and turn it into a task force to go eat lunch somewhere. Please do not do that! It is so very simple. If God can use a piece of bubble gum to save a boy's life, what in the world can He do with Timothy?

I suppose this book is almost over. I am thankful. It has been a grand experience, but I am tired of working on it! However, if I could leave you with one thought for the years to come, it would simply be 'REMEMBER WHO YOU ARE!'

Remember that you are a child of God.

Remember that you come from a long line of believers who have had all the trials, the struggles, and the joys of believers.

Remember that God has given you a spirit of courage with which to conquer life.

Remember that you have been blessed with God's spirit of power, love, and self-control.

God bless you in the days to come and thank you for reading these pages.

www.ingramcontent.com/pod-product-compliance
Lightning Source LLC
Chambersburg PA
CBHW072002110526
44592CB00012B/1182